Tall Tales and MisAdventures of a Young Westernized Oriental Gentleman

BOOKS BY GOH POH SENG

Fiction

If We Dream Too Long (1972, 1994, 2010)

The Immolation (1977, 2011)

A Dance Of Moths (1995)

Dance With White Clouds (2001)

Tall Tales and MisAdventures of a Young Westernized
Oriental Gentleman (2014)

Poetry

Eyewitness (1976)

Lines From Batu Ferringhi (1978)

Bird With One Wing (1982)

The Girl From Ermita & Selected Poems (1998)

As Though The Gods Love Us (2000)

www.gohpohseng.com

Tall Tales and MisAdventures of a Young Westernized Oriental Gentleman

by GOH POH SENG

RIDGE BOOKS
SINGAPORE

© 2015 Goh Poh Seng

Published under the Ridge Books imprint by:

NUS Press
National University of Singapore
AS3-01-02, 3 Arts Link
Singapore 117569

Fax: (65) 6774-0652
E-mail: nusbooks@nus.edu.sg
Website: http://www.nus.edu.sg/nuspress

ISBN 978-9971-69-634-4 (Paper)

National Library Board, Singapore Cataloguing-in-Publication Data

Goh, Poh Seng, 1936–2010.
   Tall Tales and misadventures of a young westernized oriental gentleman/ Goh Poh Seng. – Singapore: Ridge Books, c2015.
   p. cm.
   ISBN: 978-9971-69-634-4 (pbk.)

   1. Goh, Poh Seng, 1936–2010 – Childhood and youth. 2. Singaporeans – Ireland – History – 20th century. 3. Asian students – Ireland – History – 20th century. 4. Authors, Singaporean – 20th century – Biography. 5. Novelists, Singaporean – 20th century – Biography. 6. Poets, Singaporean – 20th century – Biography. 7. Ireland – History – 20th century – Biography. I. Title.

PR9570.S53
S823 — dc23   OCN786447190

Cover design: Kajin Goh

Printed by: Markono Print Media Pte Ltd

To

Kio Kee
Johnny
Xian

Contents

Acknowledgements

FIRST, WE WOULD LIKE TO THANK Canada Council for the grant in 2000 which made the writing of the novella *Cloch na Rón* possible. Our thanks also to George McWhirter, former head of the Creative Writing Faculty at University of British Columbia, who first suggested to Poh Seng that he should write about his student days in Ireland, and who kindly read and edited the manuscript in 2006.

Excerpts from *Cloch na Rón* have been published in *Strike the Wok* (Canada: TSAR Publications, 2001) and *Viewfinder: Tales from the Global Village* (Germany: Langenscheidt, 2007).

A Star-Lovely Art was published in *Moving Worlds — A Journal of Transcultural Writings* 10, 1 (2010) — "Reviewing Singapore".

We would also like to thank Robin Tenison for permission to publish the story *Chez Tenison* and the late Richard Adenay, executor of Tom Pierre's estate, for permission to publish *The Reinvented Man*.

Our thanks also to Matt Risling and Nadia Chew who gave so freely of their time in helping Poh Seng with his work during his last years.

The Goh Family
Vancouver, September 2014

Foreword

THIS IS BY WAY OF BEING an invitation to enter the charmed and serendipitous world of Poh Seng's young manhood, the years of his rites of passage and self-discovery. These were the years of the fifties, which he spent mainly in Dublin and the Irish countryside, sent there by his family from Malaya to be educated as a doctor. The pieces offered here present not so much a memoir as memories transformed by the artist's imagination into self-contained but interlinked short stories. The nine stories all reflect Poh Seng's extraordinary gift for friendship, and centre on remarkable individuals who almost all in unusual ways had broken the mould, and opened Poh Seng to new possibilities and perspectives. The thread which runs through all of them is the awakening of his young imagination and love of words, not only the discovery of his vocation as writer and poet, but also of the irresistible force of this vocation.

It was Poh Seng's great good fortune that his father enrolled him not in England, but in Blackrock College outside Dublin, where he would earn the academic qualifications to enable him to enter the University College/Dublin medical programme. The first of the stories, "Passage to England", presents a marvellously evocative account of a 16-year-old's ocean voyage from Singapore to Southampton. But Southampton and London were only way stations. Poh Seng's real spiritual and imaginative passage was to Ireland — with its painful history of subjection to English rule, and its heroic record of fighting for Independence, and, more importantly, its cultural autonomy and self-realization. Poh Seng's arrival in Ireland coincided with increasing turmoil in Malaya and Singapore, which culminated in the successful drive for Independence.

Naturally, he and many of his fellow students shared in the stirring emotions of the time which were so well understood in Ireland. In Poh Seng's case, these feelings led him to find his voice as a writer. Coming from a family which had struggled successfully to establish itself in Kuala Lumpur over two generations, he carried on his shoulders his family's dream that he should be a doctor, and he clearly had the mental powers and devotion to people to be an excellent one. However, he gradually came to understand that a flair for writing was far rarer than a talent for medicine, and that for "every thousand doctors there could only be one writer." The stories that follow trace his discovery of this insight. While he surely sympathized with Patrick Kavanagh's comment, "the role of the poet in society, the function of poetry in the cause of nationalism, all these sound false to me", emerging countries like Singapore and Malaya urgently needed their young writers to find a voice, and express in some way the common experience.

Poh Seng's coming to Ireland in the fifties was an unusually lucky chance, because Ireland at the time was the home to a literature with a global reach and resonance. As a young man, he was a devourer of books, and he particularly admired the gritty realism of such writers as Sean O'Casey and James Joyce, and the carnival *joie de vivre* of J.M. Synge.

However, the two writers who most deeply influenced him were the ones with whom he had personal encounters: Patrick Kavanagh and Samuel Beckett, each in his own way a giant of modern literature. These encounters are recorded in two of the most memorable stories in the present collection, "A Star-Lovely Art" and "Do I Dare to Eat a Peach?". The greater influence was undoubtedly Patrick Kavanagh who befriended him, and could be described as the foster father of his first uncertain steps as a poet.

Beckett also played a significant role in his self-discovery as a poet, providing a tremendous jolt to his sensibility at a critical moment, and becoming a considerable influence particularly on his earlier writings. The nature of the jolt becomes clear in his account in "Do I Dare to Eat a Peach?" of his response to a very early Trinity College production of Beckett's *Endgame*. The unquenchable laughter and tears which left him "drained and elated" marked him deeply. Who would not have been moved by Beckett's depiction of the laughable human grotesques stumbling their way through life under the Damoclean sword of something like a nuclear winter: the two most human of them, Nell and Nag, stuffed into trash cans, and bravely popping up every now and then, only to be slammed down again and again into their dark prison. In one of his earliest poems, he describes a Dublin newsboy as living in "a contracting cage", and this sense of the many different kinds of figurative cages in which human beings get themselves trapped gives force to the strong compassion which underlies the pictures given in his novels *If We Dream Too Long* and *Dance of Moths* of individuals in Singapore struggling to escape from, among other things, the crippling effects of themselves. Under the aura of Samuel Beckett, it would not have been surprising if he had turned to writing the kind of symbolic drama which represents man as "the nth Adam", not rooted in any particular community, and which speaks to all human beings.

However, his friendship with Patrick Kavanagh, recorded in "A Star-Lovely Art", turned his mind in a different direction. Kavanagh was frequently dwelling on the fact that even living in Dublin was for him a kind of exile: in Kavanagh's words from "A Star-Lovely Art", "speaking for myself, I should have had the guts, the integrity, to live where I was born ... I should have stayed among my own people, unique and special, the dirt poor farmers of Monaghan. And to be a poet and not accept this true source of inspiration is as bad as to be a poet, and not know his trade."

A version of these words must have engraved itself on Poh Seng's mind, for when he had taken up his vocation as a writer and graduated from medicine, he returned to Singapore as writer and doctor to care for his own people and record their experience in plays, poems, and novels. In these, he more than occasionally wrote of those whose creative wings had been clipped, and whose hopes had been stifled by dire circumstance: at its most extreme, in the picture he gives of the father of one of his protagonists, "the universal small man who no longer knew how to claim or clamour for his own uniqueness … A submissive subjugated man, who had accepted his fate, had accepted the dictates of the government, the police, his employers, his superiors" (*Dance of Moths*: 53).

There is a curious paradox in these Irish stories of Poh Seng's. On the one hand, they point to his discovery of his call as a writer to faithfully record the crippling and confined (though sometimes comic) reality of ordinary people caught in the traps of oppressive circumstance or exploitation. On the other, almost all the central figures in them have in one way or another risen above oppressive circumstance to assert their own uniqueness and creative power. This is as true of "The Reinvented Man", Tom Pierre, from a lower class black family from Trinidad, who weaves around himself a myth of aristocracy, style and elegance, as it is of the passionate American red-headed girl who sits on spray-swept wharves to paint fishermen and strides into strictly "men only" bars to stand a drink for every man in the place and sing out the toasts "To Connemara, God bless Connemara!" and "To Ireland, may God bless Ireland!" It is equally true of Patrick Kavanagh making extraordinary poetry out of his dirt poor Monaghan childhood, as it is of the aristocrat Ruth Tenison, breaking up the crust of her world with her delight in writing children's books, and her pleasure in creating a warmly inclusive atmosphere at her elegant dinner parties where those with fiercely opposed political and artistic perspectives can meet with gentleness and courtesy. Each of these stories in its own way is filled with a sense of the amazing possibilities of life, but these possibilities are always grounded and facilitated by the liberating effects of friendship.

It is not surprising that in these stories, Poh Seng should have chosen to write about those who rose above circumstances, because in 1995, he needed to rise above circumstances in his own life. 1995 was indeed a dark year for him, the year when he was diagnosed with Parkinson's disease, and when he learned that he might not be able to continue to practise medicine. Ten years earlier, the Rainbow Lounge, Singapore's first disco and live music venue, which he had founded, had closed down, essentially because of its boundary-pushing tendencies. As a consequence, among other things, of heavy financial losses occasioned by this, Poh Seng decided to emigrate to Canada. One of the redeeming features of his exile was that it eventually took him to the wild and comparatively isolated shores of the great island of Newfoundland where he practised medicine in the small outport community of Cow Head for a couple of years. Here he was close to a world of crags and cliffs and pounding seas as well as long stretches of sheltered sandy beaches. His closeness to this elemental world and the warmth of the welcome he received must have called back to his mind the idyllic days in a similar region — coastal Connemara — during his time many years earlier in Ireland.

Thoughts of Newfoundland and Ireland must have recurred to him after he returned to Vancouver to live, perhaps particularly so at the time when he received the bad news about his illness in 1995. It seems natural that the shock of a dismaying diagnosis and the likely ending of his medical career compelled him to face his own mortality, and to turn his thoughts back to the time of his genesis as a man and a writer. Both the medical necessities of treatment and the creative excitement and cosmopolitanism of the city must have held him in Vancouver, but the pull of the Canadian East Coast and no doubt the affinities between Ireland and

Newfoundland were very strong, and in the summer of 2001, he returned to Newfoundland.

By this time, he had already begun to conceive of the idea of a sequence of Irish stories. For years, he had been telling his friends tales of his student days in Ireland. Then in 1999, when he finally became reconciled to the fact that he would never again work as a doctor, he began working on a substantial novella *One Summer at Cloch na Rón* (included in this collection). This jogged his memory about the experiences with all the friends he had made in Dublin during the fifties, and so, following completion of the novella, he set down to work on what was at first intended to be a novel based on his Dublin experiences, but then became a sequence of short stories. One of the main reasons for this was that the Parkinson's from which he suffered affected his sequential thinking and memory, and so he found it easier to cast his fictionalized experiences in the shorter and more discontinuous form.

I first met Poh Seng that summer of 2001. It was a difficult and painful time, because his dear friend Al Pittman, the poet and dramatist, was gravely ill. On the day I first met Poh Seng, Al had only a week to live. In many ways, Al was to Newfoundland writing what Patrick Kavanagh had been to Irish. Poh Seng and I had barely shaken hands before we were assisting an extraordinarily weak and frail Al into the car, and together, with many stops, we drove Al to the haven which had always been a refuge to him, the publisher Clyde Rose's little house at Crawley's Cove in the Gros Morne country, where a small circle of Al's closest friends had gathered. I remember that Poh Seng and I were unable to carry Al into the house, and that in the absence of a stretcher, his friends carried him slung in a fishing net. When Al had settled, a circle of his friends gathered around the bed and sang for what seemed like hours a variety of Newfoundland and Irish songs: surely in the hope of giving Al a sense of homecoming to a place, where forever in Al's words "the dancers are stepping it out/on the floorboards of their spindrift dreams" and "the water lapping at the land-wash will lull us to sleep" ("Another Night in Crawley's Cove"). This shared experience, harshly punctuated a week later by Al's death, was of the kind that marks one for life, reminding us of our fragility and reinforcing the drive to make a creative response to life's cruelty and capriciousness. I know that this was true for me, and I am sure that it was also true for Poh Seng, strengthening the impulse in him to write of his beginnings as a writer.

For the next seven years, Poh Seng lived during the summer months near the mouth of the Bay of Islands on Newfoundland's West Coast, first in a rented house, and then in one he and Margaret had bought in the fishing outport community of Lark Harbour. This was the perfect place to write and revise the Irish stories. From the kitchen, you could look over to the sheltered harbour (no doubt similar to the one in "Cloch na Rón"), and out to where the Bay opened out into the Gulf. At one side of the house, there was a shed much like a summer house, where every morning soon after dawn Poh Seng would go to work on his writing. His routine was governed by an almost monk-like discipline, though his was certainly a labour of love. His experience in the little shed must have brought to mind the idyllic cottage at Loughbawn, which Ruth Tenison had offered him as a retreat for writing ("Chez Tenison"). As he writes in this story, "my love for cottages, huts, sheds, and cabins … was a lifelong affair."

The little cabin gave him a retreat, a place for the detach-ment necessary for writing, but there were also aspects of isolation. He and Margaret were far from any great centre (though they did winter in Vancouver). They did not have a car, so for necessities and groceries, they had to ride the mail truck in and out of Corner Brook, 30 miles up the bay. One is reminded here of the account given in "Cloch na Rón" of Poh Seng's ride out to the Trimbles' cottage in Nick Gallagher's lime green Anglia van, stuffed with the carcasses of sheep and pigs.

Their home became a place of friendship and hospitality. There was a fairly constant stream of visitors, neighbours from Lark Harbour, fishermen, café owners, teachers, and friends from Corner Brook, many from Memorial University. There were also writers, artists, scholars, publishers, painters, students, instructors, and professors. Their hospitality extended to offering visitors mouth-watering dishes, often lobster, crab, halibut, codfish, scallops, sometimes made more piquant with tangy spices and sauces. Maybe these were recipes derived from the Nonya and Baba cooking, referred to in the "Passage to England". I know that they made dining in Lark Harbour a savoury experience. At their house, there was a celebration of good food, which is so important in the life of Singapore and Malaysia, and which is decidedly reflected in the Irish stories, where moments of stress, loneliness or celebration are often marked by the experience of culinary pleasure.

Lark Harbour was also the place where Poh Seng could indulge his love for the natural world, especially the sea. I still have a picture in my mind's eye of him unsteadily making his way out into the salt water over hard pebbles (his Parkinson's was steadily getting worse from year to year), and suddenly flinging his sandals to shore and plunging into the frigid water, just as he had in the episode recorded in "A True Blackrock Boy" (though by now he was inured and even enjoyed icy waters). No sooner had he come back to shore and warmed up than he would suggest a walk, and we would make our way along the firm sand at the high tide mark, sometimes glimpsing the flashing black and white of an osprey's wing hovering high over the bay, and sometimes following the darting movement of little peeps (sandpipers) along the foreshore. One of the walks of which Poh Seng was particularly fond was the one over to Cedar Cove where there were huge jumbles of driftwood, including trees with thick trunks that had been torn from the earth. Another walk took us out towards the Virgin Mary ponds along a narrow laneway that sometimes wound through marshy ground, and where, along the fringes, we tried to spot delicate orange-tinged chanterelle mushrooms (to be taken home and cooked for dinner). Often on these walks, Margaret would gather leafy sprays or smooth and beautifully shaped pebbles to be painted with the shapes of sea creatures.

A special place we visited in the fall was Lark Harbour's cemetery on a small hill, with its scattered white crosses overlooking the community and the sea. As we made our way through the matted grass and vegetation beside the graves, we would see numerous globes of dark crimson, countless partridgeberries, which we would gather to make into jam. Maybe it reminded Poh Seng of the lonely cemetery on the Connemara coast (described in "Cloch na Rón") where he first discovered: "that afternoon, at the cemetery by the sea, I felt like a poet. I felt equal to it. I understood that to make a poem, I must enter into a state of innocence."

I believe that in the last years of his life, Lark Harbour provided him with a deep sense of home: a place to which he and those dear to him could always return in their dreams and imagination. He and Margaret were never so happy and elated as when they were anticipating a visit from their sons Kasan, Kagan, Kajin and Kakim, their daughter-in-law Camilla, and their grandchildren. Somehow the place offered an elemental connection to family, friendship, feasting, delight in the wild beauty of the natural world and the deep fulfilment of writing. It was the perfect place to flesh out the sequence of stories that recorded the experiences that had made him into a writer, and which were to impel him to return to Singapore and Malaysia, and rediscover the true source of his inspiration.

Martin Ware
Professor of English
Sir Wilfred Grenfell College
Newfoundland

Passage to England

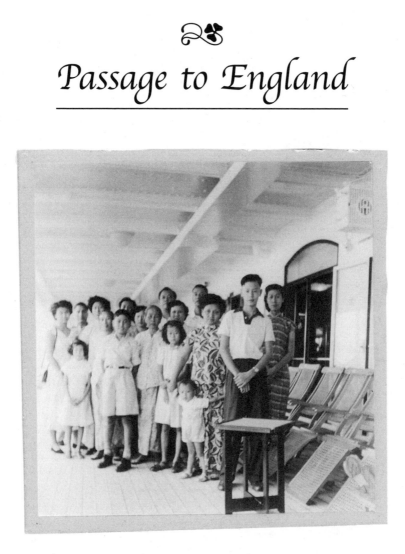

I WAS JUST A SMALL CHILD when my paternal grandfather passed away. Before he died, he had expressed a wish to my parents that he wanted me to have a university education. Although an illiterate immigrant, he believed that education was the most valuable asset a man could possess. Sacrifices had to be made if necessary. So at the age of 16, it was decided that I should study in Ireland. This was a grave and costly responsibility which made a big dent in the family budget and in April 1953, I embarked on the journey from Singapore to Southampton on the Dutch liner, *M.V. Oranje*, with a great load on my shoulders.

The day of my departure was made significant by the large number of family members who had come down all the way from Kuala Lumpur to see me off: my two grand-mothers, numerous aunts and uncles and a horde of cousins. The news that I was to study abroad had spread quickly, and for weeks our house was abuzz with excitement. I would be the first in my family to study in Europe. Everyone wanted to be involved in the preparations for this great adventure.

The night before I sailed, there had been a memorable dinner at a Chinese restaurant in Singapore. My father ordered roast suckling pig and sharksfin soup. Later, back in the small hotel, the adults sat around and talked about their dreams for me. I was exhorted to take good care of myself, to study hard and to make my family proud.

The next day, the whole family descended on the *Oranje*. We were stunned by the grandeur of the ship and examined every nook and cranny. We had never been on a passenger liner before. The *Oranje* was magic, like a city afloat.

Finally all the well-wishers were off the vessel. As the ship sedately separated from land, I realized that I was really leaving home.

My cabin mate was Sonny Yap whose mother was a family friend. Our parents had arranged that we should travel together. When I went down to the cabin, Sonny was already ensconced on the lower bunk, leafing through a magazine. I climbed onto the upper bunk and soon fell asleep. I awoke, feeling a bit disoriented for some moments in that unfamiliar setting. Through the port hole, the sky was blazing white. The ship was so quiet and steady, it seemed not to be moving at all. I got up.

Sonny was not around. Someone had slipped a note under the door. It contained the ship's programme: the time of meals; seating arrangements in the dining room; advice to keep valuables in the Purser's office. We were also informed that the ship was sailing due north that day, plying the Straits of Malacca to reach Palawan on the northern tip of the island of Sumatra sometime in the early evening. We would not be going ashore, the ship mooring outside the town so that additional passengers could be ferried out by small craft. We were to depart the following morning.

I went up to the promenade deck. The sea was all around, the only hint of land eastwards, where the Malay Peninsula was situated, a dark shadowy rim of green. It was calm, the ride incredibly smooth. It was only when I leaned over the railing and looked down that I saw her bow cutting a swathe through the greyish-green water. Yes, I was being taken away slowly from my home. What awaited me there in that far distance?

I felt alone that afternoon. We passed the occasional ship. Nearer shore, we saw elegant Indonesian *prahus* and Makassan junks with their tall masts and traditional rigging, unchanged for centuries, carrying cane and camphor.

That night, we had been requested to dine in full suit. Sonny and I shared a table with an elderly Scottish couple, Mr. and Mrs. MacDuirmud. The husband had just retired from a small trading company in north Malaya. Our other dinner companion was a young Dutch geologist, Hans Reoult. The Scots were a bit stiff and formal, and polite to the two young Asiatics at their table. Such obvious greenhorns, awkward and uncomfortable in their new suits, their startled looks and obvious bewilderment. The geologist was friendlier. Sonny at 19 and me at 16 were woefully ignorant and had little experience in social intercourse, especially with Europeans. I was painfully aware of my attire, my tie was strangling me. Conversation was stilted and sluggish; for long stretches, we maintained an uneasy silence.

"So you are going to Dublin?"

"Yes, sir!" Sonny and I chimed, like good little boys.

"The Irish, of course, are a strange breed. You'll get on well with them if you profess to hate the British as much as they do! Hating the British is an Irish national pastime ..."

"Perhaps they have ample reasons," Hans offered.

"True, true. The British didn't treat the Scots any gentler. They took from us, they did. Our historical relationship with the British is scarred with betrayal and bitterness. Still, it would not do for us to sow the seeds of discontent, of hatred, amongst these young men. I believe the British Empire on the whole has benefitted the Asiatics to a large extent. I know what I am speaking about. My wife and I have been in these parts for more than 30 years. We saw Singapore's economy prosper under the Union Jack. Indeed, if not for Sir Stamford Raffles, Singapore would not have existed."

Sonny and I did not quite know what to say. We sat in silence as if the conversation had nothing to do with us. Yet something stirred, seethed in me.

"My husband is absolutely right, of course," Mrs. Mac-Diurmud contributed. "We have both seen at first hand the good wrought by British rule. Compare that to the barbaric Japanese!"

"And you Hans, don't you think that Dutch rule has improved the quality of the life of the Indonesians?" Mr. MacDiurmud asked, sipping from a tumbler full of Scotch whiskey, and taking a pull at his cigar. He blew out a stream of white aromatic smoke.

"Me, I don't really know," the geologist shrugged, taking the easy way out.

It was a relief when dinner was over and we dispersed. There was dancing in the ballroom. Others headed for the bar. I made my way to the upper deck drawn outside by the warm tropical night. I was not aware that the ship had anchored while we were at dinner. I would have liked to have watched the operation. I was eager to see everything. In the near distance, the lights of Palawan glittered.

On my way back to the cabin, I stopped and watched the dancers. The band was made up of six white musicians in black tuxedos. Couples glided like luminous fairies across the smooth shining floor synchronous to the rhythm of the music.

❦

The dawn smelled fresh of the sea when I ventured up on deck the next morning. The crew were hard at work loading the oncoming cargo from Palawan. The metallic arms of the crane groaned from the weight of the crates that they picked up from the lighters tied alongside and unloaded them into the holds, the insatiable bowels of the ship. I stood and watched for a long while, then proceeded to the dining room for breakfast.

As during dinner the night before, we were served by Indonesian waiters. The waiters, stewards and other crew members were all Indonesian; the officers were Dutch: a socio-political reality of the times.

That late morning, the *Oranje* weighed anchor and headed towards Ceylon. According to a Persian fairytale, Ceylon was once known as Serendip. "Serendipity" — one of my favourite words, meaning "the facility to find valuable and agreeable things not sought for."

By noon, there was no sight of land anywhere. We were completely surrounded by the vast waters of the Indian Ocean. The ship had become a universe of its own, a tiny speck in the cosmos.

There was a live boat drill the next morning. We were divided into groups to assemble at specific stations next to the lifeboats, wearing our bright orange-red vests. No one took the drill seriously. I saw Sonny, waved him over. He had toured the ship scouting for beautiful girls. There were no Chinese girls onboard and the few European girls were off-limits, an unspoken convention. Prospects were bleak.

In the late afternoon, a breeze began to blow and the ocean showed white caps and endless rolls of waves. The ship continued its placid way, steady as she goes. By the twilight hour, the wind had picked up force, the waves grown bigger, and the ship began to roll perceptibly from side to side, and to plunge and lift its bow. I watched the colourful sunset, the ball of the sun dropping and then sinking past the horizon. How did they navigate this vast ocean? Perhaps the good ship *Oranje* would sail off the edge of the world, never to be found again!

By dinnertime, I began to feel unwell. Cold sweat formed on my brow. I lost my appetite. I sat at dinner, feeling miserable and green.

"Are you feeling seasick?" asked Mrs. MacDiurmud.

I shook my head. I was absurdly ashamed of my frailty.

"We're heading into a storm. I understand it will hit us later tonight. It's going to be pretty nasty," Mr. MacDiurmud reported, to cheer me up, no doubt.

"And it'll last for days," Mrs. MacDuirmud said.

"Yes, till we reach Colombo. We have the whole width of the Indian Ocean to cross, and there'll be no let up, no relief until then," Mr. MacDiurmud added gleefully. "Afraid you're going to be one sick laddie!"

"Yo, ho!" Mrs. MacDiurmud exclaimed, as if this prospect made her jubilant.

"Get up on deck as much as possible. You're likely to cut your sea legs that way," Hans said encouragingly.

I liked this young Dutchman. Lean and wiry, quick of hand and mind, like a featherweight boxer, he had reddish-brown hair cut short, standing up like bunches of arrows. Fine freckles spotted his face, which was rough with facial hair. He had spent two years working as a geologist with Dutch Shell in Indonesia. He professed to love the Indonesians and admired their rich cultural life. And Indonesia itself, comprising some 7,000 islands spread out in the archipelago, appealed to him. Alas, he added gravely, it was the Dutch he couldn't stand, his own countrymen. With few exceptions, they tended to look down on the Indonesians. Hans had a genuine regard for them and had even attempted to study Bahasa Indonesia. His colleagues disapproved, and eventually ostracized him. He resigned from his post in disgust.

I retired early, climbed up onto my bunk bed and lay down, my arms across my chest like a mummy. I could feel the ship rising and plunging. After a long while, I sank into sleep.

I woke up in the middle of the night to a world in turmoil. Everything was rolling madly. I felt dizzy. My stomach turned. I made a quick dash to the bathroom just in time to throw up into the toilet. I held my head in my hands and retched and vomited again and again. It seemed worse when I opened my eyes.

In the midst of this commotion, Sonny told me that we had hit a terrible storm. He was seasick too. I could hardly hear him. I groaned, flushed the toilet and staggered back to my bunk. There was no relief from the tossing. I wished there was just some way of stopping this torment. I was willing to do anything. I wished I had not come.

I threw up three more times that night. It was a nightmare. Came morning, the storm seemed to have gotten worse, if that was possible. A sickly grey light came through the small port hole, which jumped up and down, would not hold still. I had never been so miserable in my life. I felt really sorry for myself. I was in no state to hazard the journey to the dining room for breakfast.

The steward came in to clean the cabin. He regarded me with commiseration. As the Indonesian and Malay languages are very similar, I could converse with him in my crude bazaar Malay. His name was Ali Sastromijoyo and he was from Jogyakarta. He realized I couldn't eat and asked if I would like some hot tea. I thanked him but turned down his offer. Ali nodded. He understood.

I don't know how I survived that long day and night. I just lay on my bunk feeling weak and sick. I could only keep down small sips of water and tea. The following day gave no let up. Sonny brought back some seasick pills from the infirmary. I took them, hopefully, but my condition did not improve. I was miserable. Sonny then suggested we go up on deck as the fresh air might help. The very idea of climbing up to the deck was akin to climbing Mount Everest!

For five more endless days the ship rode the rough sea, tossing me about like a yo-yo. I began to lose weight.

One afternoon, Hans paid a visit and treated me to the gossip aboard ship. The MacDiurmuds were alas as strong as horses with appetites to match. They truly relished their food and drink. Hans agreed that the food and service on the *Oranje* were excellent. It was a pity I could not enjoy them at the moment. Never mind, he consoled. We'd be sailing into calmer waters soon. Colombo was just a couple of days away.

Land! O blessed land!

The following day, it was indeed calmer. I plucked up courage, got dressed and headed for the deck accompanied by Sonny. The sea was still rough and angry, the water grey and white. I felt weak and wobbly, but that night, I made it to dinner, to cheers from my table companions.

I had not eaten for almost a week and was hungry but I did not do justice to the four-course dinner. A big chunk of meat sat on the plate like an opponent. I was just not partial to European food.

The next morning, when Ali came in to tidy up the cabin, he was pleased to see me looking better. I told him I had attempted to eat, but the white man's food did not agree with me. I asked what kind of food he and the crew ate and found out that part of the ship's kitchen catered Indonesian food for them. Beef Rendang, Soto Ayam, Sayor Gadoh, Nasi Gudek! My mouth watered. Ali laughed and proposed that he bring me some curry and rice. I nodded eagerly. So it was arranged that Ali smuggled food to me daily. Ali saved my life. He was tickled-pink that a passenger would request Asian food, and with a touch of pride, refused any money.

So I went to the dining room only to socialize. I played with the food set before me. The MacDiurmuds teased that I ate like a tiny mouse. If only they knew!

Sonny sniffed the air in our cabin one day and thought he was hallucinating. He swore he smelled curry. I laughed, and divulged my secret. After that, the two of us ate in our cabin happy as can be, Ali fussing like a mother hen. He was delighted when we ate with bare hands, the common practice in Southeast Asia. Oh, how we stuffed ourselves. I wondered how on earth I was going to survive for the next few years on alien food!

I looked forward eagerly to Colombo in Ceylon, our first port of call. It would be the first time I set foot on foreign soil. As the ship docked at the busy harbour, I recalled weekends at my grandmother's house in Kuala Lumpur. The adults would gamble at mahjong and poker, the radio tuned to Radio Ceylon for the dance music of Joe Loss, Victor Sylvester, Perez Prado, Xavier Cugat and his buxom wife, the gorgeous Abbe Lane. It had taken about a week to sail from Singapore to Colombo and I marvelled at how technology could relay the music through all that distance. There was so much for me to learn.

Ceylon was also known as the "Pearl of the Orient". For centuries, adventurers had visited its shores. Marco Polo came in 1293. The legendary Sinbad the Sailor was said to have stopped there. From the 15th century, the island was colonized first by the Portuguese, then the Dutch and finally the British. It had just become independent in 1949.

Hans, Sonny and I joined a bus tour. Colombo had many similarities with my hometown, Kuala Lumpur. Because of the climate, the same palm and flowering trees, and because of our colonial past, a similar architecture in the civic buildings. My most enduring memory of Colombo was a visit to the Church of Saint Francis Xavier. I had never been in a church before, and the lofty ceiling, the dim, cool space, the smell of incense and the silence made an impression on me. The tour stopped at Mount Lavinia Hotel situated on one of the most beautiful beaches on the island. I took off my shoes and strolled along the beach, the fine sand between my toes. The hotel treated us to a sumptuous array of Ceylonese curries at lunch.

Back on the ship, I joined a group of fellow passengers watching a throng of local vendors hawking their wares. I had been warned that these vendors were skilled bargainers who could extract money out of the most resistant onlooker. I was confident that no one could cheat me so easily. I watched, amused. One hawker caught my attention. He grinned at me and shouted, "Sir, sir, please buy this beautiful elephant. I give you cheap, a present for your son or daughter!"

"But I've no son or daughter!"

The people beside me laughed.

The vendor was delighted. He had managed to establish contact, however tenuous, with a potential buyer.

"Oh, sir, this you can keep, for sure. One day you get many, many children. You such a strong man. You need many elephants. You buy this baby elephant and the mother elephant and the papa elephant. Please, sir, keep this elephant family happy. You have a good heart I can tell."

"No, thanks. What will I do with a carved elephant?"

11

"Oh, elephant bring you good luck, this we Ceylonese believe. It will also give you strength," and here he mimicked the thrust of the act of coitus.

Again, everyone laughed.

"I don't want to buy anything," I contended.

"Please, sir. Have pity. My wife and six children are starving at home. We have nothing to eat. Please help us. Buy just this small elephant. Going cheap sir. I give special price for you."

"No, thanks," I said, with a note of finality. I was beginning to congratulate myself for coming out unscathed.

"Going cheap, sir. Like gift. Only 15 dollar!" a hint of desperation in his voice, his quarry was getting away.

I shook an adamant no.

"You name price, sir!"

I thought I would stop all this nonsense once and for all by offering a ridiculous figure.

"Six dollars!" I yelled back.

"Sold!" the man said.

So I ended up with a black carved wooden elephant, my souvenir from Colombo. The workmanship was rather shoddy. I set it next to my bunk and in time became attached to it. When I lost it a few years later, I grieved a bit inside. The reasons for our attachments are sometimes mysterious.

Early that night, the *Oranje* moved away and entered the Arabian Sea. It was a relatively calm stretch to our next destination, the port of Aden at the entrance into the Red Sea. With the food from Ali, I had regained weight at the rate of a pound a day. I began to enjoy the trip, participating in shipboard activities such as shuffle board, chess and checkers, and dance classes. I made a few more acquaintances. We accepted the fact that onboard ship, relationships were shallow and transient, lasting for the duration of the journey, probably never to set eyes on one another again. Our paths crossed for awhile, that was all.

I had a good time although I can't recall much of what I did. The only book I read on the trip was *Oliver Twist*. As

I would be spending two days in London before proceeding to Dublin, I wondered whether London would be as sordid, dark and cold as Dickens had described. Hardly a city to look forward to.

The days grew hotter and hotter as we crossed the Arabian Sea and I took to wearing short pants and short-sleeved shirts again. Still, I sweated. Our small cabin was stuffy, even with the port-hole widely opened. The heavy air covered us like a blanket.

We reached Aden in the middle of the day. I watched with curiosity as we docked. We were under a different sky, more white, and a different landscape of sand and rock. The date palms and other scrub vegetation bore a different green, with a patina of grey, from the foliage in Malaya. The people were also different, Arabs going about in their traditional garb, the *kafeyeh*, with the women covered from head to toe. I was fascinated. It was the geography lessons in school coming alive. I was disappointed that we were unable to disembark. The *Oranje* was here only for a few hours.

Then we made our way up the Red Sea. The seawater wasn't red at all, but the same blue-grey. However, at sunset, the sea did turn red with the sun sinking into the flat horizon. I thought of Arabia, the land of fables, of caliphs and minarets, harems and camels, of Ali Baba and the 40 thieves, and Scheherazade, especially Scheherazade, and her tales from the Arabian nights, who spun stories because her life depended on it. O the romance of it all! I wanted to set foot on this land so filled with wonders. The land of Pharaohs, of pyramids and sphinxes, one of the oldest civilizations of mankind.

That night, a festive line of revellers danced the conga from the ballroom out onto the open deck, I amongst them. A crescent Muslim moon and myriad stars winked at us. I felt so fortunate to be here on this ship, on the Red Sea.

Later that night, unable to sleep, I crept up deck to watch the coming of dawn, and the immortal lines of FitzGerald's translation of *Omar Khayyam*, haunted and enchanted me:

Awake! For Morning in the Bowl of Night
Has flung the Stone that put the Stars to Flight.
And Lo! the Hunter of the East has caught
The Sultan's Turret in a Noose of Light.

I felt intense joy. I imagined myself coming upon Ozymandias in the vast desert sands, and the words of Shelley:

Look on my works, ye Mighty, and despair!
Nothing beside remains. Round the decay
Of that colossal wreck, boundless and bare
The lone and level sands stretch far away.

These poems best depict how I had felt that magical night, even before I knew I would write poetry.

We sailed up the Suez Canal to Port Said. We had learnt in school how ships from Europe once had to sail round the Cape of Good Hope in Africa to reach Asia. The Suez Canal shortened this voyage considerably and facilitated the growth of trade. But I was not impressed with this great engineering feat. The canal was just a gash of water through the desert. There was nothing to look at except sand stretching into the distance.

Everything changed after the Suez Canal. We entered the Mediterranean Sea. We were now in Europe! At once, it became cooler, reminding us that we had left the Tropics and entered a different climate. The ship seemed to move perceptibly faster, with intention. Everything became faster. Time, it seemed, had also sped up.

Onboard the *Oranje*, a number of events were organized to mark the last stage of our voyage. The culmination was the Gala Farewell Night. The dining room and the ballroom were festooned with lights and decorations. The crew and the passengers turned out in all their finery. The captain exhorted us to celebrate the end of our journey before dispersing to our separate destinations. We were leaving one another after three weeks of confined togetherness, back to our different lives and different fates.

The very last afternoon, Sonny and I wanted a final dip in the pool. To our shock and horror, the water was too cold. This was springtime. How would we survive the winter ahead?

Soon, we passed the massive rock of Gibralter. We had a straight run to Southampton. As we neared England, each day got colder and colder. We bade farewell the night before we reached Southampton. Hans said we should write to each other, that he would be interested to find out how we fared in Europe. He had good intentions, but no one, including Hans himself, really believed that we would contact each other again. Looking back, I do not think that I forged any meaningful or lasting relationships with anyone during the voyage. The *Oranje* had brought us together for three weeks. That was all.

We arrived at Southampton in the early morning. It was cold and dark and raining. A black wind blew. Added to the strain of disembarking, and immigration and customs clearances, it was not a cheerful welcome. Finally, we boarded the train.

The ride to London was a sad disillusion. From the train, all we saw were grim and broken backyards and derelict buildings. Maybe the war had done this. I felt let down, cheated. This wasn't the city or land of my dreams.

Worlds within World

ONE MOONLESS AUGUST NIGHT, I danced the slow foxtrot with Lily Foo at Raglan Road, an event organized by the Malayan Student's Union in Dublin. Truth be told, it had not been much of a party. For some reason, there was no life to it. The very air bred boredom. The dancers could not be coaxed to execute the flash and verve of inspired dancing. Those with other options began to slip away relatively early. Throughout the evening, more and more guests departed, floating silently away like ghosts. The ones who remained behind had the forlorn look of the abandoned; an evening wasted, they hung around like vagabonds. I too, stuck around, because I had nothing better to do.

So there I was, with a girl in my arms, doing a little smooching, but stealthily, a thief I was, of love. Something warned me that I should not trifle with Lily Foo. I chose to ignore it. After all, I was holding her in my arms. It felt very agreeable.

This may be the moment to bring Emily Chin into our story. Emily was not my girlfriend. She wasn't even my date, formally speaking, for this dance party. It just happened that all of us were boarding at Mrs. Angela Kennedy's. No. 21 Raglan Road was a hostel exclusively for students from Malaya and Singapore. I was fortunate to be allocated a single room there. My parents had booked ahead so that my accommodation was secured during those first weeks of strangeness and confusion in Dublin, where I had come to pursue my studies.

Mrs. Kennedy's husband had been a senior police officer at the British-run Internal Security Department in Malaya. When Noel Kennedy retired, they returned to Dublin and bought a large comfortable house in Ballsbridge, a well-to-do section of the city. A dozen or more young students boarded with them at any one time. It was especially suitable for those away from home for the first time in a foreign country. The hostel had a familiar, homely atmosphere, and Mrs. K, as she was affectionately called, was ever ready to lend a sympathetic ear.

Definitely a great draw was the food, for Mrs. K, bless her, offered Malayan home cooking from her kitchen. Although not totally authentic, not like the Malayan cooking we were used to, we could kiss her feet for making it possible for us to eat curry chicken, fried rice, etcetera, etcetera. It is well known that food ranked number one for all Malayan and Singapore students. We cannot live without our local Nonya and Baba cooking.

During the early days in Dublin, from the safety of Mrs. K's, I made forays out to the world at large; each time a little bolder. I was still suffering from terrible homesickness, and I missed my family sorely. But I was also enjoying those idle days of a gorgeous summer, bright and spacious, and marvelled at the contrasts to life in Kuala Lumpur. Even the grass was of a different green in Ireland.

Yes, Dublin was a lovely city, although it was not London, the centre and capital of the British Empire.

Now, all I had seen of London were some famous landmarks and historical buildings. A city steeped in the past. It made me realize my own lack of a palpable history. Malaya was not an ancient, civilized nation with a proud past. We were only a young colony.

After a 23-day sea voyage from Singapore to Southampton, my cabin mate and fellow traveller, Sonny Yap and I, had taken the train to London. We were to spend two days there before travelling on to Dublin. At Charing Cross Station, we stood dazed and lost, surrounded by a pile of luggage as the other commuters milled around us. Then we saw a man holding a placard with our names.

He approached us. "Sonny Yap and Poh Seng Goh?" he enquired. "I'm John Heywood from the British Council. Learnt from the KL Office re: your coming today. Right on the spot!"

"How very nice of you," Sonny and I chirped.

"We have booked you two single rooms at the Queensway Hostel."

John Heywood took charge, instructing two elderly porters to take care of our luggage. Two taxis were needed for the mountain of suitcases and bundles we had brought with us. I had no idea of the contents of the bundles but guessed they contained foodstuffs. My family had heard about the rationing of food in Europe after the war and was afraid I might starve. The bundles were all firmly tied and sealed, probably to discourage HM Customs from examining them too closely. Strange smells emanated from some of them. Probably Malayan delicacies not available abroad.

Those two days in London, Sonny and I dashed about like headless chickens. We took photographs of each other standing in front of Buckingham Palace, the Eros statue in Piccadilly Circus, feeding the pigeons in Trafalgar Square and the ducks in Hyde Park. These were later developed and sent home, testament that we had made it safely to our destination.

Spring was in the air and we felt it in Hyde Park near the Serpentine where we witnessed our first live kiss. Before this, we had only seen screen kisses in the movies. Now, a couple on a park bench were actually kissing in public!

The water in the Serpentine was a filthy brown, and we were shocked to learn that people swam there in the summer. The numerous wild ducks here and the pigeons in Trafalgar Square were a source of wonder. If this was KL, their population would have been obliterated overnight, and many homes would have roast pigeon or succulent duck gracing their tables!

We also came across a number of monuments dedicated to generals and admirals who had fought in one war or another. There they stood, looking rigidly ahead, with a formidable martial air. How the English must love wars to have so many military heroes. We had heard their martial march music on Pathé News in the cinema. At school, we were taught to sing:

> Some talk of Alexander, and some of Hercules,
> Of Hector and Lysander, and such great names like these,
> But of all the world's great heroes, there's none that can compare,
> With a tow, row, row, row, row, row, to the British Grenediers

By the time we left London, we were foot sore from all the walking and sightseeing. However, we had no regrets. London did not disappoint and I was resolved to visit again. I suddenly felt fearless and independent! I would be an adventurer, a wanderer: master of my own fate.

We flew by Aer Lingus to Dublin. The plane was green in colour and I imagined it floating calmly in the sun above the spring green fields of the Emerald Isle, and felt a happiness welling within. That morning, I inducted green as my favourite colour.

Mrs. Kennedy's establishment was a home away from home. Everyone was friendly and helpful, especially in those early days when I was a greenhorn in this new city. The other boarders acted as my guides, taking me around; advising me which restaurant served good cheap food, which grocer to shop at, which café had the best ice-cream, coffee, afternoon tea and scones, the nearest and friendliest pub, although I did not imbibe alcohol then, which shoe shop, haberdashery, and which butcher to patronize, who would give away free pork bones, chicken necks and feet, items considered choice bits by us, but which the Irish were not keen on.

The boys persuaded me to buy a new coat, saying I would need it against the cold. So one weepy and grey-sky morning, five of my compatriots from Raglan Road bundled me onto a green Number 10 bus and we went to Cecil Gees downtown. I bought a long coat made of gabardine just like the one that each of them was wearing. We strolled out of the shop together in a solid bunch, and catching our reflection in a shop window, I thought we looked like a gang of Mafiosi out on a rampage. A fedora would have been perfect with our get-up. Alas, the fedora was out of fashion then. Instead, our hair was plastered with Brylcreem, which was the fashion of the early 50s. Everywhere we went, the heavy scent of Brylcreem trailed behind us.

Those four months at Mrs. K's were a gift. I enjoyed having all that time of my own, without plans, timetables or schedules. I did not have to explain or apologize to anyone. I was my own free man. Perhaps I did feel a little bit guilty. It was all those exhortations in the letters from home, my parents urging me to work hard, and put that quiet time to good use. There was always something more useful I could do, such as study Latin. So I took out my Latin books and read Caesar because I was a good boy. Most of the time, though, I lazed about.

The other residents at Mrs. K's were good company; we went about everywhere in a group: to the cinema, the ice-cream parlour, window shopping, Phoenix Park, and nearby resorts like Dún Laoghaire where we walked out along the stone and concrete arm of the harbour, and on excursions to Bray, Glendalough and Powers Court.

One Saturday in late summer, the leaves still green as can be, we chartered a van that seated 20 and headed south for Howth Head, about an hour outside Dublin. There was a sandy beach and a noted bird sanctuary at an adjacent small island called Ireland's Eye. As we strolled through the small village, a gang of youngsters followed us and chanted:

Jap Jap Jap Japanese
Jap Jap Jap
Filthy Japanese.

It was a harmless incident, I know, but the fact that we were singled out because we looked different, galled me.

That was the very first time I had encountered discrimination because of colour or race.

We saw a great number of films, indulging ourselves like starved children. Our taste was non-existent; we belonged to that fabled lowest common denominator said to be responsible for all that is trashy in the cinema. A set of twins from Ipoh town, Robert and Rodney Chin, dubbed the Chin Twins, inducted us into the delicious world of eroticism and pornography. They had an enviable collection of picture books which we read breathlessly in our rooms behind locked doors. It's hard to believe how low I had sunk in just four months! The Chin Twins were masters of corruption. May they thrive in every hostel!

In the balmy summer evenings, we gathered in the sitting room, to chit chat or gossip, or listen to the Chin Twins telling dirty stories, and we were wracked with laughter at their funny dirty jokes. Then the girls would bring their movie magazines and the latest pop records. We listened to, and sang along with Doris Day, Rosemary Clooney, Bing Crosby, Nat King Cole and, of course, Frank Sinatra. Also Johnny Ray, Frankie Lane, and Julie London, whom the boys drooled over. All in all, we were a happy bunch. With so many of us in the house, it was like a perpetual party.

Mrs. K set up some cooking sessions in her kitchen for the benefit of those who could not cook. She warned that we might need such skills before long. The boys were more interested in the cooking sessions than the girls. It was a surprise to me, for at home, when Ah Foon Cheah, our *amah* who ruled the kitchen, offered to teach me, I absconded. The general belief was that women ran the kitchen, and it was considered sissy for males to cook. Now, in Raglan Road, I learnt that more boys wore the apron than the fair sex, a reversal of tradition, of social mores.

Indeed, the young women professed that they had never spent any time in the kitchen, that they had never learnt to cook. Lily Foo once asked me to teach her to boil water. Her older sister Peggy asked for assistance to ascertain if her eggs were cooked. I am not sure if they were only pulling my leg. There was a lot of school-girly giggling.

I found out that the Foo sisters had been our neighbours in Treacher Road, Kuala Lumpur, although we had never met. I had biked past their bungalow every day on my way to school. Their father was reputed to be a rich man, the owner of a shoe factory. "Kum Foo" shoes were economical and hardy and very popular in KL. Lily was his favourite daughter.

The other pair of sisters at Mrs. K's was Betty and Emily Chin, not related to the male Chin Twins. Their mother turned out to have been a close friend of my mother when they were both young girls in Kuala Kubu.

That sociable summer, there were often parties at Mrs. K's. The parties were usually small, just the boarders and a few invited guests. Non-alcoholic punch, soft drinks and tit-bits were served. There would be some beer for the few older students and guests. A small dance floor was created by rolling up the carpet and moving the heavier furniture aside. We danced to recorded music from a big old gramophone.

One rather late night, I was dancing a slow number with Emily, the younger of the Chin sisters. Influenced by the slow, sensual romantic music, our young bodies drifted naturally close. I felt a pair of pert little breasts against my chest; her warm cheek was smooth against mine and then I felt our loins melding together. It was spontaneous, auto-matic and unplanned. We stayed rubbing against each other. I had a rise. We danced like that much of the night. It was exciting and devil may care. I ground and ground and Emily reciprocated defiantly.

The next morning being a Sunday, Emily went with a bunch of friends to mass. I wondered whether she went to confession that week.

"O Father, Father, I had impure thoughts and indulged in sinful acts!"

In actual fact, Emily was neither scrupulous nor a prude. She was intelligent and level-headed and the best-looking girl at Mrs. K's that year. Everyone thought highly of her. That summer, we nearly drifted into a boyfriend-girlfriend status. We held hands occasionally in the cinema, but that was that. I did not even kiss her once, although she seemed ready for it. We never necked. We were in no hurry. Did not want to rush into a real commitment. We could wait.

Then came the party in August. By 11, there were only a few couples dancing. Earlier on, I had danced with Emily most of the time. As there were more girls, the men were encouraged to circulate. So I thought I was doing my duty when I invited Lily for the last dance. The lights were switched off, and two red candles gave off a feeble light on the side table. Lily and I danced a number of fast dances, working up a sweat, our hearts thumping. I was enjoying myself. When the tempo changed to a slow dance, our bodies pressed against each other, as if drawn by some irresistible magnetism: the natural pull between male and female. We were tangled in the vicarious mating dance of the species. Caught in the throes of our bodies, we continued to dance, mesmerized. A kind of passion took over. I realized that the Lily I was holding in my arms was different from the Lily I had known before. That Lily had been shy and restrained, pure and vulnerable; her father's precious daughter, his little darling. Who could have believed it would be so easy to open her up, to do this!

I thought I glimpsed Emily at the periphery of my vision, and danced away. A moment later, she had vanished. A little disconcerted, I wondered if she had gone to bed. I continued dancing with Lily Foo.

The next morning at breakfast, Emily glared at me disdainfully and ignored me. I knew she was angry but felt I was under no obligation to her. I had made no promises, had not pledged my feelings in any way. I could dance with anyone I wished. I had played within the rules.

In time to come, Emily and I became quite good friends. Much later, she fell in love with and married a medical student from Formosa.

It was different with Lily. She was sitting all alone in the dining room. I nodded to her on my way to the serving counter. After I had filled my tray, I walked past her and sat alone at another table. I don't know why I did that. Perhaps I did not want any complications.

Lily was still alone when I finished breakfast. As I walked past on leaving, I thought Lily's eyes were moist with incipient tears. In the days that followed, Lily walked about with a bruised look on her face and I assiduously avoided her.

Then Lily left! Suddenly! All sorts of conjectures floated about. Finally Peggy, her older sister, clarified the situation. Lily was not happy in Dublin and had asked her father to send her to the medical school at Harvard. We were all impressed: the Harvard Medical School! Peggy informed us that Lily had been the star pupil at St. Mary's Girls' School in Kuala Lumpur.

For some time after, I fancied I smelled a charred odour in the air about me: the burning of innocence.

The whole atmosphere at Mrs. K's began to change for me. I sensed the other students talking about me, saying that I was a scoundrel who played hard and fast with the girls.

For my part, I began to feel claustrophobic. Mrs. K's had become too small. The company of only fellow Asian students was becoming too confining. We hardly ever mixed with anyone else in Dublin. Surely meeting people of other cultures and backgrounds was why we were sent abroad to study — to broaden our minds, our horizons. We were keeping too much to our own kind. I longed to break free. I resolved to be fearless. I would step forth unto the great world.

A True Blackrock Boy

AT THE END OF SUMMER, I BECAME A BOARDER at Blackrock College. Blackrock was a small village by the sea, situated on the outskirts of the city, on the way to Dún Laoghaire and Bray. I was enrolled in the Fifth form, equivalent to the standard at my school at home in Kuala Lumpur. This meant that I had an entire two years before I could sit for the Irish Matriculation. It was a long scholastic road to being a doctor.

Life at Blackrock College was woefully different from living at home, enfolded in the warmth of my family. From the very first day, I realized that I was to be incarcerated within that jumble of grey stone buildings, joyless and grim. No more freedom to go about as I wished. Yes, the clanging of the gate at the end of day also marked a farewell to the joyful days of my youth. I had entered a life of restrictions that would be strictly administered. The program for each day was cast in solid and unmalleable stone. We, the hapless student body, were controlled from the moment we were awakened by the loud and raucous ringing of bells, to the switching off of the lights and imposing of sleep in the dormitory.

Sharing a dormitory with 40 Form Four and Form Five students, there was absolutely no privacy. The first few nights, I cried bitterly and secretly at my circumstances. Occasional sniffles in the silent night suggested I was not alone.

Our day began with early Mass in the school chapel, followed by breakfast in the big dining hall. In a few short weeks I learnt to wolf down my food, that in a dog-eat-dog world and if I didn't learn to fight for my share, I would have no breakfast at all! And breakfast, I found, was the best meal of the day, usually bread, baked in the kitchen and named "rock" bread for obvious reasons. There was also oatmeal and milk, butter and jam, and strong tea. Nothing fancy, just good, plain cooking.

Then it was off to classes until lunchtime. Lunch was the heaviest meal of the day but appalling food. Day in and day out, it was so bad that eating became torture, not pleasure. I ought to explain that the preparation and consumption of food are regarded by every true Malaysian and Singaporean as the highest art form, each meal not just simply gobbled down but devotedly tasted and passionately praised or condemned. The culinary reputation of a family's table often determines its social status. Social standing rests on what issues from the kitchen. One can understand the terrible impact the unpalatable and unaccustomed food had on me, coming from this background.

One time, the students attempted a protest. Their stand consisted of a partial hunger strike. The ringleaders issued ultimatums and there was great excitement. Inspired by Mahatma Gandhi, they also declared that their actions would remain non-violent. I can recall the dark face of Sam Juveri, shining with passion for this cause. Sam was incandescent, the chief spokesman for the student body.

Representing the other side was Father Donovan, the small, wiry and razor-sharp Dean of Studies, soft-spoken and articulate. Without a doubt, a power in the College. He broke up the whole brouhaha when he walked to the microphone and announced, "I'm taking this strike seriously and will try to redress things. For instance, I'm going to support your partial hunger strike by instructing the kitchen to prepare only half portions for each student. This will be in effect from supper this evening. The College thanks you for your charitable act. It's exemplary of the best tradition of Blackrock.

For your information, the food saved shall be sent to the needy and the hungry. We intend to send it over to the St. Vincent de Paul Mission."

The assembled student body burst into laughter and applause. They appreciated a good victory, even at their expense. So this student action crumbled. Life returned to normal. We continued to eat rock-hard bread and unidentifiable meat, if not with gusto, at least in good sport.

Later in life, whenever I recalled the unsuccessful hunger strike at Blackrock College, I remembered the flashing face of Sam Juveri, arms raised like a revolutionary, battling the ills and injustices of our imperfect world. Many years later, in 1973, I met Sam again, when we both were invited to attend an Afro-Asian Writers' Symposium held in Manila in the Philippines. Our reunion was warm and genuine, almost two decades after we were young students in Dublin. Sam was limping badly and had to use wooden crutches to move about. He told me a ghastly story. He had returned to Malawi after his studies, eager to play a constructive role in nation-building. There were so many ills and so much backwardness in every sector that needed patriotic attention. Unfortunately, his liberal and ethical views ran counter to those of the government under Dr. Hastings Banda. He was taken into custody by the Internal Security Forces and severely beaten. His right leg was broken in several places as a warning of much worse things to come should he persist in voicing dissent to the ruling regime under that megalomaniacal and egotistical dictator. Concerned, I urged him to be careful. He only laughed, an incandescent smile spreading across his face. A year after the Symposium on Revolution and Literature in Manila, I read a report that a writer from Malawi, Sam Juveri, had again been detained by the government for an indefinite period.

Apart from the meals, our studies made up for the greater part of the day. Recess after lunch and after tea were the only free times we had for recreation. After tea came night studies, when we revised or completed our work under the supervision of one of the priests. Then it was time to get ready for bed, and all too soon, the brother in charge of the dorm would float through to check that all was well, so quiet and smooth his passage he might not have been walking on the ground, but levitating.

The early weeks were the hardest to bear. The rigid, boring and joyless schedule caused a chronic listlessness. I dreaded each grey day. As time slowed to a crawl, I suffered from a surfeit of sameness to my days. I often wondered, bitterly, during those long, wintry months, whether my parents realized that they had, in reality, committed me to a prison and at great cost! I contemplated complaining to them about the real Blackrock, that it was a far cry from the impressive and polished brochures and prospectus. But I did not have the heart to worry them, knowing full well the heavy financial sacrifices they were enduring on my account. It had been my own wish and my own dream to explore the great big world outside the small one in Kuala Lumpur. So I communicated by aerogramme, once every fortnight as mutually agreed. I always reassured them that everything was fine, that I was grateful to be sent overseas for my studies. All patently untrue.

Another peculiar practice at Blackrock was the weekly mass bathing. Back home, it was customary to bathe at least once a day because of the heat. In the English colonial school which I attended, we had been taught that cleanliness was next to godliness. At Blackrock, bathing was restricted to once a week. On bath days, we boys were marched to the bath house. Its low ceiling was criss-crossed with a network of pipes with small showerheads fixed at intervals. In charge of the whole operation was a Brother known as the Bath Superintendent. The boys were made to strip and then wait as batch after batch were given a signal to take up position under the showerheads. The Bath Superintendent would then open the main tap control, releasing small sprinklings of barely tepid water down upon our heads. We learnt to soap and cleanse our bodies quickly as we had been warned that the shower would be on for only three minutes with strictly no extensions. Inevitably, some of us would not have completed our baths when the water was shut, and pathetic wails would rise with the steam. These half-soaked, half-soaped specimens would appeal to the vested authority to no avail.

"O Brother! Brother! Some more water please soap's smartin' me eyes. Please, a bit more hot water Brother for the love o' God!"

Such pleas were never successful. We learnt to beat the clock, finishing our showers in under three minutes flat. If we could not do so, we learnt to ignore the malodorous smell clinging to our bodies until the next bath, and on certain warm nights, the wafting of a cloud, faintly green, would float above us in the dorm, bearing the accumulated smells of some 20 partially cleaned bodies.

The highlight of our days in Blackrock was undoubtedly our one Sunday off each month. This was a delight beyond measure. In actuality, we only had half a day, because of High Mass in the morning. It would often be 11 o'clock by the time we were released. Nevertheless, to be released for part of a day, to ride the green double-decker bus into Dublin town, looking keenly out of the window at the passing scene, the long, westward facing Bay of Dublin extending towards Howth Head, the whole sea a dull grey, was a pleasure we all looked forward to. I would wonder about the distinctive Martello Towers rising at intervals along the beach. I remember that the sky above Sandy Mount, a neighbourhood of small houses, seaside cottages for the lower middle class, was always grey, never sunshiny. How we enjoyed and treasured those free days. We marked these days in red on our calendars.

As part of the recreational programme, there was a cinema show every first Sunday of the month. We looked forward to these shows eagerly. Among features shown that year were "The Song of Bernadette", "Winchester 73",

"Treasure of the Lost Canyon", "The Apparition of the Lady of Fatima", "Morning Departure" and "Never Take No for an Answer".

When the weather turned cold and wet and daylight shrank, resulting in some curtailment of outdoor sport activities, the College arranged musical evenings. It was part of their charge to bring culture to our souls and to groom us into gentlemen. I must admit that at first I fell asleep at most of these functions. They regularly featured guest singers and musicians, many of whom were obese, with girths like wine barrels. I was bored beyond endurance.

Then one evening several weeks later, a miracle took place. A man of great size began to sing. He sang in German, which I did not understand, but the beautiful music moved me profoundly. It was such a wonder, to be able to make such music. O the ingenuity and creativity of man. Later, I learnt that he had been singing some of Franz Schubert's Lieders.

However, the principle cultural event of that year in Blackrock was the College production of the operetta, the "Mikado" by Gilbert and Sullivan. Father Donovan was the musical director as well as the conductor of the school orchestra. As an Asian, I should have been offended by this absurd caricature of Japanese life, but I was won over from the start by the zest and jollity, humour and charm of the operetta.

Immediately, I fell in love with Yum Yum, or rather with the young boy who played this leading female role. To me, he was more beautiful and desirable than any girl I had met. I did not experience any feeling of wrongdoing over this puppy love. Incredible as it seems now, up until then, I knew very little about homosexuality. I was so ignorant and protected at 17!

For weeks, I went about the school grounds humming, even singing the catchy song:

Oh, I'm going to marry Yum Yum, Yum Yum!

I affected a smitten look every time I crossed paths with the 13-year-old actor, or would it be more correct to say "actress"? I remember how he had looked at me with a coquettish smile, although he was probably giving this smile to half the student body, all hopelessly smitten with unrequited love and forbidden wishes that year at Blackrock.

As the weeks went by, I began to discover other activities as a boarder, and even grew to like them. I especially enjoyed watching rugby and became a fervent supporter of the school teams, the JCT and the SCT, the Junior College and Senior College Teams, in the series of interschool matches leading towards winning the annual competition, the all-important Annual County Championship Cup. As usual, our main rivals were two other premiere schools, Conglowes and Belvedere. The three schools had long been locked in a series of arduous battles, the keenest of which had become part of the annals of legend. Blackrock College dominated the Annual County Championships. The true Blackrock boy was fanatical about school rugby, and I became a passionate convert to the sport. The entire student body, all the Fathers and teachers as well as the domestic staff, were mad about rugby. Blackrock was one enormous, collective rugby fiend. At matches, we became one compact entity, decked out in our dark blue blazers with the College crest, long blue and white striped woollen scarves wound round our necks and the regulation caps. We would go forth in solidarity. Thus primed, we supported our teams with delirious and mad enthusiasm. It was a thing to behold.

1953 was a vintage year. We had, as captain of the SCT, a great wingman, the celebrated Niall Brophy, our tall hero, big, statuesque, with the might and speed of Apollo. Watching him leading charge after charge into the enemy's turf, his determination conspicuous in the fray, making a run on the flanks, was magical. He was also a stout defender, ready to die out there in the field, under the sun or rain, under our very eyes. Yes, even to death! What a hero, what an inspiration to the assembled thousand Blackrock boys, mesmerized by his breathtaking feats.

We also had Johnny Woods as scrum-half. Johnny was a favourite of mine: small, wiry, quick and elusive as Mercury, snatching a loose ball from nowhere and making his lightning run, his bolt from the whole mass of players, into the very heart of the foe, to score right there, under heaven. Our Johnny the cunning, who infused the game with his poetry time and again.

And the rest of the team were immortals to us. How we cheered and shouted at the top of our lungs, sang rugby songs till we were hoarse, till we lost our voices, till we were delirious. I know I shall always remember the rugby songs and the cheers all my living days!

> *Rock boys are we!*
> *Our title is our glory,*
> *Fearless and bold*
> *Whatever the danger be,*
> *Onward we go*
> *To flinch and falter never!*
> *Rock boys together,*
> *The Blue and White forever!*

Or we would chant as one:

> *Rock a boo, rock a doo*
> *Forward for the White and Blue*
> *R O C K*
> *Rock forever!*

Or when one of our chaps was brought down brutally in a rough and foul tackle and lay writhing in pain on the green field, we would all console him:

> *Old soldiers never die,*
> *Never die, never die,*
> *Old soldiers never die,*
> *They only fade away!*

I shall treasure my memory of the day we won the SCT Finals at Lansdowne Park. After the match, we commandeered the small district train back to Blackrock, singing, clapping and laughing, delirious with joy. It was the most wonderful day in our lives!

⨯

I did well in my studies. Indeed, I seemed to have enjoyed them. I liked English classes in particular, and looked forward with keen anticipation to those conducted by Father De Vertuile, whose passion for literature infected me. Father De Vertuile often got me to read my essays aloud. Eventually, I won the English prize, quite a notable achievement for one whose mother tongue was not English.

One day, towards the end of the school year, Father De Vertuile asked me whether I had ever thought of becoming a writer. Seeing the puzzled look on my face, that kind man told me that he thought I had the gift. He added that this was bestowed by God and was rare. He knew I had intentions to study medicine and added that for a thousand doctors, however worthwhile they may be, only one could become a writer. He made me feel very special. I had harboured no such notions, but the seed was planted.

My good performance in studies fed my ego and self-esteem. I also won prizes in other subjects.

Sometime during my second term at Blackrock, I informed the Principal, Father Hampson, that I was keen to become a Roman Catholic. Arrangements were then made for me to study Catholic doctrine and scripture. My spiritual teacher was Father Maibeen. This step enhanced my status with the teachers and won me some special privileges. For instance, the Principal and the Dean of Studies informed me that I could go to the nearby village of Blackrock to catch a movie whenever I wanted, but I was advised to be discreet and not boast about it to the other students. No student had ever been granted this dispensation before as far as I knew. All these additional privileges, and especially the conspiratorial secrecy that went with them, made me feel I was party to something unethical. So I never took advantage, never went to a movie in the village.

Alas, the doctrinal and spiritual studies were deadly dull, with poor Father Maibeen trying his best to explain to me the mysteries of the Holy Trinity and the Immaculate Conception of the Virgin Mary. I never truly understood and/or believed in what that poor man was so passionately trying to teach me. We had frequent but friendly arguments that frustrated my teacher. I knew this had reached the point of discomfort, if not uneasiness, for him. During pauses, he would march up and down the room like the soldier that he was, the priest being the soldier of Christ. Father Maibeen would then fetch an apple and invite me to relax while he tried to communicate with me by playing the violin. He quite believed that this strategic manoeuvre would help to unclog the blockage interfering with my understanding of the mysteries of the Church. From then on, each time I was given an apple or other fruit from the large basket sitting on his polished hardwood table, Father Maibeen would also fetch his violin and play a piece by Mozart or Brahms. He was quite an accomplished musician and could speak eloquently through his violin. However, I was there not to learn music but to truly understand the scriptures and to believe in them through my spiritual studies. It was crucially important for my entry into the Church. We never solved this impasse.

Finally, I was willing to be baptized, but deep inside, I suffered some anguish as I never fully accepted or understood his teachings. And so at length, I carried my doubts with me into the Church.

⁂

When the Easter holidays came round, I decided to stay behind in school rather than spend the time in Dublin. I asked permission, saying that I wanted to apply to my studies without the distractions of city life. This again flummoxed the school authorities, for no other student had ever made a similar request in the past: to remain in school at holiday time. Initially, this unusual request was turned down because of lack of precedence. I persevered and eventually it was agreed that I could stay behind at Easter.

It turned out to be a most excellent arrangement. It was April and the beginning of Spring, my very first experience of this season in a temperate climate. Back home in Kuala Lumpur, there was perpetual heat and humidity, an unchangingness of weather, whereas in Ireland, I was able to witness the true progression of Spring, the intensification of light, the lengthening of the days, the awakening of life, the greening of the earth. Birds returned, flower buds burst into bloom. This fascinating thaw of winter brought an end to the cold and the darkness, and soon, memories of the snow melted away.

With the departure of the student body from the school, universal silence and peace settled in my world like a gigantic bird. I could now stroll along the long corridors without colliding with other bodies, hear the resonance of my own footsteps. I could sit alone in the dining room without being jostled, and enjoy my meals at leisure. And the meals were uncommonly good! The domestic staff fed me well. I would never have imagined that the same kitchen staff who had supplied all our meals at term time, could treat me to such fare. A miraculous transformation, no less! Now, I even looked forward to meal times while previously they were only to be tolerated.

I was served tender roast beef with delicious gravy, baked fish with chips, and even the boiled cabbage was edible! I never could have dreamt that there was anything beyond bread pudding for dessert. Now, I was served apple pie and ice cream, peach tart and chocolate mousse. It was as if I was staying in a luxury hotel. I found out I was being served the same food as the Fathers. Boy, I thought, they sure eat well, pledge of poverty notwithstanding.

Even attending chapel was an enhanced treat. It was easier to concentrate in that cloistered, vaulted space without the presence of the whole student congregation. In that quiet and stillness, it seemed I could draw nearer to God. I did not have to share Him with so many other people. I liked this privilege.

Between bouts of study, I strolled the ample grounds, the many playing fields now empty, the old orchard at the back, and many of the lawns and flower beds colourful with Spring blossoms. When the weather turned distinctly warmer, I brought my books outdoors, lay on the grass in the sunlight and studied. It was a pleasant experience, and I was glad about my decision to stay behind in school that Easter break.

One particularly hot mid-afternoon, I was lying on a grassy patch by the verge of the main playing field, the scene of many exciting and victorious rugby matches, when a tall figure in a black cassock strolled towards me. It was my English teacher, the young Father De Vertuile. A warm smile lit up his face.

"What are you studying?" he asked.

"Milton, Father."

"Don't you think it's too glorious a day to be parsing *Paradise Lost*?" he teased.

"I guess you're right."

"Do you find Milton difficult?"

"He's not easy. But I like the texture of his writing, and when reading him out loud, it's like chewing a rich tasty meal. And, if I may say so, quite sensual."

We chatted a little while about Milton, and he offered some nuggets of critical appraisal. Then he invited me to join him for a swim at the Baths Pool down in Blackrock village. It seemed an agreeable idea and I eagerly accepted his invitation. We went to fetch our swimming togs and towels and then proceeded to walk across the playing field, down the main drive and through the front gate; the big wrought-iron leaves of the gate lay open. We then turned right and walked down the sloping road that led to the village of Blackrock.

The road accorded a view across the bay to Brayhead on one side, and across to Howth Head on the other. It was indeed a lovely day.

On the way, Father De Vertuile pointed out a Martello Tower on the coast, a tall, cylindrical stone structure of grey granite. Similar towers were erected at intervals along the bay as defence structures. Buck Mulligan, in James Joyce's *Ulysses*, lived in one of them.

"Have you read Joyce?"

"No, Father, not yet."

"You know, don't you, our Holy Mother, the Church, considers it an evil and blasphemous book. Other people as well. It has been banned in many quarters for its obscenity ever since it first appeared in 1922."

"I have not read him."

"Oh, you probably will one day. You probably should if you are going to be a writer."

"Why, Father?"

"Because of its seminal place in the development of modern literature. Many people consider it a great book."

"Do you, Father?"

"Me? Well, it's denounced by the wisdom of our Holy Mother, the Church, as an evil and blasphemous work. Don't forget that. But, yes, I think it's a great book. But that's only my own opinion. You, I advise, should follow the Church's ruling."

"Isn't that hypocrisy?"

"Not necessarily. In your case, it could be construed as humility."

It's no wonder I had so much respect and affection for Father De Vertuile. That bright afternoon as we made our way down to the Baths, I couldn't wait to read the infamous *Ulysses*.

It was my first visit to the Baths. There was a small concrete and brick building where the changing rooms, showers and toilets were located. We purchased our tickets at a booth.

The nearby sea was blue and inviting. Packs of white sea-gulls glided past, squawking and turning their round, luminous black eyes, to survey the sea. The pool itself was quite small, filled with salt water pumped directly from the sea. There were not more than half a dozen swimmers. Father De Vertuile and I changed, locked our belongings in the lockers and emerged at the poolside.

"Can you swim?" the Father asked me.

"Yes Father. In my old school at home, a premier school, we have our own swimming pool. It's called the Victoria Institution."

"One can easily tell it must have been a good school judging by your scholastic performance."

I was gratified to hear this compliment. I valued his opinion.

The sun was at its apogee and I wasn't feeling cold. Only my bare feet felt the cold wet floor, but that didn't bother me.

"Here we go!" Father De Vertuile shouted, and plunged into the deep end of the pool.

"Here we go!" I too shouted, and plunged into the water.

I received a nasty shock. The water was freezing cold. Not what I had expected. I had never experienced water that cold in my life. It was physically painful. My body felt numb. When my head resurfaced, I let out a loud scream. I struggled in the water and had difficulty breathing, the air so cold I could hardly draw it in.

Father De Vertuile swam towards me and asked, "Are you alright?"

"C-c-c-cold! C-c-c-cold!" My teeth chattered like clicking castanets. My one wish was to get clear out of that tormenting pool of icy water.

Father De Vertuile could not help laughing, but said mildly, "We'd better get you out of the water. Get you into warm clothes."

With his help, I made it to the side of the pool and climbed up the steps. Once out of the water, my body began to shake. A couple of small boys looked at me in amusement.

"If you are alright now, I'll swim for a bit. Go and get dressed. Can you manage?"

"Y-y-y-yes," I stammered, and shivering uncontrollably made my way to the changing room. I had some difficulty in putting on my pants. When I finished dressing, I went to sit on a bench facing the pool, still visibly shivering for a good while. I sat all hunched up with my arms hugging my chest to keep warm. What a stupid nit I was to presume the water was the same like back home, simply because the sun was shining that day. So naive and ignorant. It was hard to believe. Sometimes, one can be stupid about the simplest things.

When we got back to school, Father De Vertuile saw to it that I was given a cup of hot chocolate in the kitchen. Of course, in the goodness of time, I became acclimatized to the changing seasons, and if I should go swimming, I know I must first test the temperature of the water by dipping a hand or foot in first, not plunge in headlong on mere assumption. Yes, look before I leap.

A Star-Lovely Art

I FIRST MET PATRICK KAVANAGH by chance when we both shared a tiny table at the Coffee Inn, a popular establishment off busy Grafton Street. This area was crawling with undiscovered writers, artists, actors and dancers, and their hangers on. Dilettantism was rife.

I was one of the small numbers of foreign students in Dublin at that time. We were conspicuous and exotic, like rare orchids, or some such thing. There were advantages and disadvantages, obviously, but this is not the moment to consider the issue. Suffice it to say that I felt different, accepted my difference, if not to exaggerate it. This had contributed to my becoming an outsider. Also, I considered myself a poet, although I had not yet written anything. I was somewhat self-conscious about this, as if I had made a wrong claim. I felt the thrill of mutual recognition whenever I was with another poet. I believed then that a poet was a special person, although I would be hard put to define just what this specialness consisted of.

So that mid-afternoon when Patrick Kavanagh came into the Coffee Inn and took a seat at my table, I was so overwhelmed, I became speechless. Of course, I recognized who he was, one of the finest living poets in Ireland. The man who called poetry "a star-lovely art"! Just think, I was sitting across the table from a true master of poetry, a man I venerated. Such a god-given opportunity to have a heart-to-heart talk with this live angel of a man in the flesh, but I was struck dumb, only able to mouth inane small talk. That brilliant, profound conversation I had wanted to conduct with Patrick Kavanagh remained only in my head. I was so ashamed. What must Kavanagh think of me? An idiot for sure!

It was a laughable situation. For the two of us to sit in such close proximity and not address each other would be unnatural. So we did talk, but only about the weather, where we came from, and other inconsequential titbits. It was obvious that he was bored. I yearned to open, to reveal myself and my poetry to the poet. I was sure that he would understand me.

I studied Patrick Kavanagh closely that afternoon, throwing stealthy side glances at him now and then. The place was packed, the collective voices trapped in that small room made conversation difficult. One had to shout, to raise one's voice, in order to be heard. It even affected one's brain, making thinking difficult. That may be part of the reason our conversation was rather laconic.

The most noticeable feature about Paddy was his hat, which sat on his head all the time. It was a brown, battered thing, time-worn, sharing all the vicissitudes gone through by its owner. Like a pet dog, it followed him around loyally. I found it peculiar that he kept it on his head all the while he was in the Coffee Inn and I wondered whether he kept it on all the time, even to bed or when bathing. My curiosity was piqued as to what his head really looked like beneath his hat, the structure and shape of it, its physiognomy. And his hair. Was it plentiful and untidy, or thinning? Was he going bald?

Another peculiarity were his eyes which were somewhat obscured by the reflecting quality of a pair of cheap plastic spectacles. Behind the lens, his pupils swam about like fish in a fish bowl in their encumbrances of water. In spite of this, his eyes could penetrate deep into your soul. So you suspect.

He carried a two to three days' growth of beard, which looked a little rough to the touch. His clothes were crumpled and a little threadbare.

When Patrick Kavanagh spoke, his voice was rough and gravelly, as though he had chronic laryngitis.

After about half an hour or so, Paddy took his leave. I stood up stiffly and formally shook his hand. I felt a little absurd and could not help feeling dissatisfied with myself. I looked after his retreating figure as he stepped out into the mild sunshine and was swallowed by the traffic. I sat down again, musing on our meeting. What a waste to have let such an opportunity pass, and to spend precious time mouthing inanities when I could have bared my soul! I don't think I even gave the poet my name. He continued to know nothing about me!

❧

Dublin was still a small city then, and it was easy to bump into friends on the streets. In the months following that first encounter, I met Paddy again accidentally three or four times. Whenever I greeted him, he would turn to me and ask, "Do I know you? What's your name?"

Each time, I was put off by this rebuff, and went away thinking: "It's your loss, you arrogant bastard!"

One time, I was reading at the Coffee Inn when Paddy entered. I stood up to greet him. He seemed to be in a hurry and brushed me aside. My face turned as red as a beetroot, and I spent the next hour devising devilish ways for his demise. An hour passed. I felt a hand on my shoulder. It was Paddy. He said, "Sorry, me lad. I was grappling with the muse, you see."

Then, one late summer afternoon, I was relaxing on one of the colourful canvas chairs at St. Stephen's Green, watching the world go by. I was guffawing at Myles na Gopaleen's column in the *Irish Times* when I saw Paddy approaching. He was alone, moving slowly through the pedestrian traffic. Never daunted, I went to greet him, full of trepidation. Why did I torture myself for this bastard? It was because he was a fine poet and his poems celebrated the ordinary in our mundane life:

A road, a mile of kingdom, I am king
Of banks and stones and every blooming thing.

Paddy was making his laborious way, head bent, and looked weary and in pain. I greeted him and he acknowledged me after a second's hesitation. We stood there exchanging small talk again, until I blurted out that I wanted to write poetry. I nearly beat my chest like Tarzan, Lord of the green beast-filled jungle!

Instead of words of encouragement, Paddy gave me a disapproving, even contemptuous look. He said gruffly, "And why on earth would you want to do that? Don't you think there's already more than enough fools wanting to write poetry? Tell me, what makes you think you can write?"

One barrage following another, like machine guns, *rat-tat-tat!* I was flabbergasted, being attacked like this. I didn't know what to say. I was speechless with anger and humiliation. He must have noticed the effect on me, but still he carried on, though in a perceptibly gentler voice. A father's voice.

He quoted:

"Child, do not go
Into the dark places of the soul,

I say these things in the hope of dissuading you from a life that could be filled with pain and poverty. Take me for instance. I am often penniless, sometimes I don't have money to eat, and have to importune friends for a few shillings to get by."

"I don't care whether I am rich or poor, so long as I can write poetry."

"My God! How green you are, how juvenile, and stupid too. Think of it, our man here has no fear of poverty. Just listen to him! Doesn't care if he's rich or poor, sez he. What utter rot he's spouting. Bet you when proper hunger gnaws at your guts and the larder's empty, and your wallet too, you'd not be so casual about poverty. When you have no money for the rent, and the landlord's at your tail, and you fear being thrown out into the street, homeless, you'd not likely dismiss poverty. There's nothing romantic or redeeming about poverty. It hurts both body and soul. And poetry, why you will throw poetry out of the window if, in exchange, you can eat."

"I didn't say poverty is desirable, or that one can only write when one is sunk in poverty. I meant that a poet can write under adverse circumstances, under any circumstances."

"Is that so? This I would like to see."

"Why are you so hostile? Also, if you believe in what you just said, why do you continue to write poetry? Why don't you bloody give it up?"

Paddy gave a hearty laugh, "Testing ya, you see. Yes, you are a green one, indeed you are. Don't you know by now that one's advice is for others to follow, not for our own consumption? Why, if we only followed our own advice, we'd be far better off today instead of being so messed up."

"You're condescending, or you're taking the mickey out of me." I turned away and started walking towards the exit near Grafton Street.

Paddy followed me, saying "And you my son, your pride's too easily hurt. Must toughen up if you're going to be a poet."

"There, you are making fun of me again."

"Thin skin will not do ya any good. And you misread my intentions, which is not to hurt but to prevent ya from being hurt. I too was laughed at in my youth when I came to Dublin town, a country bumpkin. I was raised on the stony grey soil of Monaghan. That was another world altogether. I've been a cowardly exile now for many a year."

"Why do you say a cowardly exile? I would think the reverse is nearer the truth?" I said, quickening my steps.

"Are you running away from me?" he asked, changing into a merry note, a twinkle in his eye.

"No, I'm not. This is my usual walking pace."

"Well, slow down will ya. You're out-walking with an old man, with bloody arthritis in his joints, and a weak heart. Every step I take gives me pain. Slow down, if you want to talk to me."

"I'm sorry. Wasn't thinking."

I stopped and waited for Paddy to catch up. I noted he was dragging his right foot, and that sometimes he winced in pain when a footfall was particularly heavy. At times I had noticed a shadow passing over his face like that thrown by a cloud upon a hillside. Of course, there was talk in town about Kavanagh's poor health, that he had diabetes, hypertension and a bad heart. Someone should be taking better care of him. However, even in those early days of our acquaintance, I knew that one must not pity the old fella. Imagine a volcanic blast of hot burning lava erupting over you if you dare try. Yes, best keep the pity to oneself.

We continued our slow stroll. I was very proud to be walking alongside the poet, conscious of the privilege. I fancied that something of poetry-making would accrue to me somehow. I was so young and superstitious then that I believed Patrick Kavanagh would simply pass off some of his poeticalness to me, that there would be a kind of effortless osmosis, a conjunction of invisible pores, emanating from the one to the other, through the skin, through the air. That there would magically be a transference so that I would write at last the necessary poems that would give meaning to my life and my death. Poems that would shake and transfix the whole bloody universe, no less.

I asked my superior and elder practitioner of the art of poetry why he regarded exile as a cowardly act. Paddy heaved a sigh, then took a deep breath, in order to tackle this young nuisance, this foolish aspiring poet.

"Speaking solely for myself and no other, I should have had the guts, the integrity, to live where I was born. Placed there originally by an incredible act of Providence, I had to run after the imagined glitter of the city, the suspicious glamour, the fake power and glory. I should have stayed put amongst my own people, unique and special, the dirt poor farmers of Monaghan. And to be a poet, and not accept this true locale, this true source of inspiration, is as bad as to be a poet and not know his trade. And I have done that to myself, turned away from my birthplace, my ancestral land, and daily I am punished for that."

"I know what you mean," I said, exercising my temerity. "I can empathize with you, being a kind of exile myself. So far away from my home."

"Sure as sin, I wake up each morning haunted by the simplest memories. I start by thinking how it was, approaching the farm, going through the narrow lane-paths leading to it, and how crowded it was, with ripened blackberries in the summertime, the sheer overgrowth rendering the passage into a leafy tunnel, the fat black berries just about everywhere, and good for the eating, for jam-making, wine-brewing. I remember how it was like, as children, tearing fistfuls and stuffing the goodness delirious into our ardent mouths. The taste of it. And I also remember how the air dances from the grassy headlands up to the bald mountains, the wind some-times churning, turning violent, and moving like a gigantic blade, scything across the fields and meadows, the heads and stems of tall grass swaying like the sea waves, and the yellow cornfields resisting the prevailing wind, agitated, their brown tassels drooping like moustaches through the entire summer. Aye, I remember, running with a pack of village kids, running after the sheep, to dispel them across the land, avoiding the hazards which cause many a child to stumble with their hidden unevenness. Such bruised knees and elbows, and the occasional wailing from a young'un. I remember too, the smell of dung when we laboured in the stables, or played with the farm animals, the sheep and cows and ponies, and the chicken yard loud with the ceaseless cackling of the fowl, all these creatures regarded almost as family. Oh yes, I remember, I remember all this and more. To bursting!"

"Your childhood seems idyllic and rural! I was brought up in a big town and hardly related to Nature at all."

"Perhaps the setting was idyllic, but I know my childhood was almost crushed by my family's poverty. As a young child, my day was made full: attending school and doing homework, the myriad farm chores as well as housework. I worked ceaselessly but no matter how hard I tried it was never finished. When I was 13 I gave up my formal education to work on the farm. I would say my life was hard, but not more so than our neighbours."

"Yes, your early poems in *Ploughman* depicted the grim poverty of the peasant so vividly."

Paddy looked at me and recited:

"Wherever I turn I see
In the stony grey soil of Monaghan
Dead loves that were born for me."

He asked, "You have read my poems?"

"I have enjoyed your poems immensely."

I watched a smile grow into full bloom. Paddy was just like the rest of us, susceptible to praise and flattery.

"No point chasing after me my lad. I don't take apprentices."

"That's all right. I never intended to be an apprentice to you. I think that a poet must struggle alone. Discover for himself."

"What an arrogant bastard you are, bejesus! You better be good, or I'll thrash your hide till it reaches your bones!"

"I know I have not written any decent poetry, but I shall."

"Ah, so you are only a potential poet, a future poet. Then I think you should carry yourself in humble measure. But why do you come to me when you say you can do it alone?"

"For pleasure. I've come to you for the pleasure we can share in poetry."

"Let's wait till you've written some decent stuff. Then we'll take it from there."

"As I've said, I like your poetry about ordinary people and their ordinary lives which is a new direction for poetry in Ireland. Right now my country is struggling for Independence. The role of a poet in that society will be complex and dangerous."

"You talk about poetry as though it's some big Hollywood production. The role of the poet in society, the function of poetry in the cause of nationalism, all these sound false to me. I am just a simple versifier. I don't understand what you are saying. You probably will dismiss me, for the kind of poet I am has no room for haughtiness and arrogance."

I felt chastened for being so ill-mannered and boastful. To make matters worse, I really had no evidence of my worth as a poet. But I did feel like a poet and I couldn't explain it.

"My son, only time will tell what you can do. In the meantime, you're right. You alone can learn the hard way, but here we are. We must part, go our single ways."

"Well, goodbye then. I shall think of what you've said. At any rate, thank you."

"Get on with your writing. I hesitate to say good luck to ya."

He crossed down Dawson Street, and I went down Grafton Street. I felt in great need of a comforting pint of Guinness.

Over the course of the next few weeks, I pondered over Paddy's words.

❧

One night, unable to sleep, I rose and paced my room. I thought I was going crazy. After an hour or so of nervous pacing, I sat down and wrote in a frenzy. Words flew out of the air onto the page of the exercise book, myself only an instrument. I wrote burning with the creative process. When I finished writing, I calmed down and slept. The next morning, I read the two pages of verse. They were quite good. I had succeeded in writing my first poem. I felt drunk. I folded it, put it in my pocket and wherever I went, be it on the bus, or while listening to a lecture at college, I would read it, and edit it. I worked on the poem for about three weeks.

One evening at the pub, I had the audacity to show it to a friend. He seemed surprised, congratulated me, and said it was not too bad.

"What do you mean, not too bad? Is that good or bad, Goddamn it?"

"It's ... not bad. What can I say?"

"You are a lover of literature, so you must know."

"I know that there are things in it that are interesting, even impressive. And there are things that are difficult to say. It's a bit of a puzzle."

"Damn you!" I said, and stormed out of the pub. My first work of creation, and what did I do? Show it to an ape!

I carried the bloody poem with me as though it was a valuable piece of jewellery. I could have walked into the path of a bus, so intoxicated did I feel. Then the Heavens smiled on me. I met the editor of the college magazine who said he'd like to have a look at my poem. The upshot was that St. Stephen's magazine published it. My first poem which filled the sky over all the denizens of Dublin!

The day it was published, I peered surreptitiously at groups of people drinking coffee and imagined they were discussing my poem. I was so high I could have forgotten my name. Then I heard my name being called. It was Paddy.

He congratulated me, and I asked him for his opinion. He would only say, "Not bad."

I grilled him that whole afternoon, and bits and pieces of his opinion danced dizzily in the smoky air of Davy Burns. I remember, apart from "Not too bad," he really meant that it was not good. Somewhere, amongst his words was his opinion. He got me very confused. Did he mean to say "Not too bad" or "Not too good" or "Bad" or "Good" or "Not bad" or "Not good"? Finally, although my life depended on what he said, what he did say eventually did not merit my dying in the most exhibitionistic fashion. At length, another friend came and patted me on the shoulder and I did not know if it was in commiseration or admiration, but he bought me a pint. Then Paddy became very excitable and exclaimed out loud that we were going to have a wonderful night to celebrate the debut of the new poet.

Paddy took over. In the course of that night, we pub-crawled through all our favourite haunts. Once we entered, Paddy would barge his way through the crowd and, standing in front of the counter, clear his throat and announce to all and sundry that they must congratulate me on this night of my debut as a poet.

"A toast to the poet!" and some drunken fella would order a round for Paddy and myself. After half a dozen pubs, we ended up at McDaid's. Paddy repeated his performance at the counter, albeit in a slur now, but he got the message across. This time, he pulled me by the hand and pushed me in front of a skinny middle-aged woman who was perched on a folded rug on top of the radiator. She was puffing on a cigarette at the end of a long holder, à la femme fatale. She had a glass of wine in her other hand. She was obviously holding court in that corner of McDaid's.

"What did you say, Paddy?" she asked through a drunken fog.

Paddy repeated his introduction, "Goh Poh Seng is a new poet!"

"I see."

She looked me up and down, then pronounced curtly, "Too bad I can't read Japanese."

This was greeted with rollicking laughter. When it died down somewhat, Paddy rode in to the rescue, "You are wrong, Anne. Poh Seng writes in English, and his work, singular in number, shows he's got some musical talent."

The woman gave me a second appraisal, a closer scrutiny, and said, "Well then, he can't be any good."

"He has promise," Paddy defended.

Later, Paddy informed me that the woman was Anne Yeats, the painter and daughter of W.B. Yeats.

All that was in 1958.

I did see Paddy now and again after that night at the Baggot Street pub but our friendship did not go beyond what has been described here.

Paddy Kavanagh died in 1967. I heard that he was buried in his beloved Monaghan. I grieved for Paddy and imagined how glad he would have been to return to his ancestral home at last.

Now and then I would recall Paddy reading and singing:

If ever you go to Dublin town
In a hundred years or so,
Inquire for me in Baggot Street
And what I was like to know.
O he was a queer one
Fol dol the di do,
He was a queer one
I tell you.

Chez Tenison

I FIRST MET MRS. RUTH TENISON at a posh, private gallery in Dublin. It was the launch of an art exhibition. Somehow, we began talking. The name of the artist escapes me now, and to be honest, I wasn't paying much attention to the exhibition either. I had already done a quick obligatory tour of the pictures on the walls, and they elicited little enthusiasm from me. I wished it were otherwise. I would have liked to enjoy them.

I made my way back to the refreshment table where drinks were being dispensed by a helpful young bartender. He gave me a friendly and encouraging smile as I helped myself to another glass of red wine, a mellow Merlot, all in a short while, but done so in a manner that would not be noticed. In other words, it was accomplished with some skill, if not with art.

"Are you an admirer of the artist?" asked a middle-aged lady in a pukka English accent, so distinct from the local Irish brogue. It marked her as Anglo-Irish, the erstwhile masters of Ireland.

"No, I don't know the artist. Never heard of him before."

"Then how do you account for your being here?" She asked, amused, rather than in disapproval.

"I came for the free booze and the food. Frankly, I was not invited but gate-crashed. I've blown my monthly allowance and need free drinks to maintain the usual alcoholic content in my bloodstream, to keep me sane and saintly."

She laughed, a civilized laugh.

"Do you know you have a civilized laugh?"

"What do you mean?"

"I didn't really know what a civilized laugh was till just now. From now on I will be able to detect a civilized laugh from across the room."

Mrs. Tenison laughed again. She seemed easily amused. She asked if I was a student. I nodded and went on to give her an encapsulated self-portrait in five minutes flat. Shameless dog, I even declared that I was a poet. Christ, what was I fishing for, and from a stranger! Well, the upshot of this encounter was that it led to another. She invited me to spend a weekend at her country estate.

"I'm having a small dinner party on Saturday and would like you to come. I think my friends will find you interesting."

❧

The Tenisons were wealthy, upper-class Anglo-Irish gentry, with a country estate of 400 acres called Loughbawn, in County Monaghan. The estate was named after the lake. Mrs. Tenison was in her late fifties, with children older than me. Three sons and a daughter. The eldest son managed a hotel which they owned in the Bahamas; the second son was in the British Foreign Office; the youngest, Robin, who was about my age, had just come down from Oxford; the daughter was to be married to a banker that autumn. Mrs. Tenison herself had such an air about her of breeding, decorum and kindness that I found it easy to become friends with her.

I arrived by train and cab in the early afternoon. Mrs. Tenison came down the front stone steps of the house to welcome me, then introduced the very correct figure standing behind her as the valet, Bryan. In the hall, she introduced me to Jane, the housekeeper, and Marie, the French cook. It was just like the movies!

I had already been impressed as the cab drove along the neat white fence which encompassed the estate as far as the eye could see. Then the long private drive up to the house. Now I followed Bryan up the stairs to my room, my small worn cardboard overnight bag carried ceremoniously by Bryan. He kindly suggested I take a short rest to freshen up before I was shown the rest of the house and the grounds.

I washed my face and appraised myself in the mirror with the ornate gold frame above the wash basin, then made my way downstairs, walking soundlessly on the thick carpet. Bryan was waiting for me at the bottom of the stairs.

"This way, sir. Mrs. Tenison awaits you in the drawing room."

"Bryan, you don't have to call me sir."

"Yes, sir!" the chap stood straight as a flag pole.

"Have you spent time in the army?"

"Yes, sir. Served in the army corp in the desert war, and then in the Far East after the war."

"That's very interesting. You know, I am from Malaya, one of your colonials."

Bryan didn't react. By this time, we had reached the drawing room, a large gracious room beautifully furnished with antiques. Tall windows framed a view of the grounds outside. Ruth Tenison beckoned me to sit beside her.

"Would you like a drink? It's just the time of day for a cocktail, don't you think? That should certainly raise the content of alcohol in your blood," she smiled.

"A cocktail's just fine, thank you."

"What cocktail would you like?"

"I am not familiar with cocktails. Why don't you choose one for me?"

She turned to Bryan and gave an order.

"This is a lovely room. I have never been in a room as beautiful as this."

"Thank you. It's my favourite room too."

"I think I've never been in a lovelier house."

"But it's just too big. Empty room after empty room, with only ghosts from the past moving about silently. I sometimes wonder whom they are looking for."

"I meant to ask, are you related to Alfred Lord Tennyson? I thought you might be, despite the difference in spelling."

"Yes. We are related. The original Tennyson tribe had a homogenous name. There was nothing peculiar when they split to two factions, one retaining the old spelling, and the other adopting a new one, namely T-e-n-i-s-o-n. We are of the breakaway branch. Alfred, Lord Tennyson belonged to the other branch. Our branch has no illustrious ancestry. Mostly involved with the military arm of the East India Company, the colonizers of India. My late husband's grandfather was a member of the higher rank in the Company's military arm. He became the de facto ruler of a vast state in central India. Sir Richard Tenison. It was he who built Loughbawn. This was his residence in the British Isles. He was fond of India, as were many other members of the family who lived there. Without exaggeration, for them, India was their first home. Loughbawn was for home leave and retirement. Come, let me show you the grounds." She rose and I followed her out of the room.

She turned to Bryan. "Sorry about the cocktails. We shall return for them later. We are just going to amble about the front lawn. We'll keep the farm for another time."

Together we left the house and strolled about the huge front lawn with its clipped grass and pruned shrubbery. She told me that the farm had been tenanted out soon after its establishment. "The farm is largely to the north and north-west of here; the actual land belonging to the house is modest. The only one in the family who's remotely interested in running the farm, or more accurately, owning a farm, is Robin, my youngest. He has just come down from Oxford and has negotiated successfully for the purchase of an old farm in the vicinity of Hastings with his inheritance. Robin has a feel for the land. He's engaged, and will wed next autumn, depending on whether he can complete a journey overland to India and beyond. Since a child, he has wanted to be an explorer. Anyway, you'll meet him soon. I hope you'll like each other."

"What a view!" I exclaimed. It was indeed lovely on that grassy rise which commanded a 360-degree view of the surrounding countryside. The sky arched over us. In the city, one doesn't see sky so big, and air so clear and bright. What a privilege to have all this real wealth. The other side of the tracks from Paddy Kavanagh's impoverished Monaghan.

"I'm so glad to be here. And also glad that you are related to the poet, Alfred, Lord Tennyson. He's one of my favourite poets. I love the sounds in his poems. I would like to recite some lines from one of his poems for you."

Mrs. Tenison clapped her hands and cried, "How marvellous!"

"I shall recite from 'In Memoriam'. It's the sequence composed after the death at age 22 of his closest friend:

Dark house, by which once more I stand
Here in the long, unlovely street,
Doors, where my heart was used to beat
So quickly, waiting for a hand.

A hand that can be clasp'd no more—
Behold me, for I cannot sleep,
And like a guilty thing I creep
At earliest morning to the door.

He is not here; but far away
The noise of life begins again
And ghastly thro' the drizzling rain
On the bald street breaks the blank day."

"That's marvellous. You recite very well."

"I only learnt it yesterday. I couldn't memorize more than three stanzas!"

"Thank you for your thoughtfulness. Actually, I do like great-grandfather-in-law's poetry. Unfortunately, our family regarded Alfred as a mild aberration to be tolerated."

She turned towards the house. "Now let me show you around."

I followed her. She took me into the grand ballroom. The first thing that struck me were the splendid chandeliers hanging from the ceiling over the dance floor. I could imagine the myriad lights shining down on an elegant and colourful crowd of revellers. My imagination ran away as usual and I fantasized dancing with a beautiful partner under those artificial stars. Next, Mrs. Tenison showed me to the billiard room. I could visualize the gentlemen, elegant and suave in their dinner jackets, smoking cigars, russet brandy twirling in their free hand as they sank a ball or in-offed the yellow into the mid-pocket.

My hostess told me that the most interesting part of the house was the museum. When we toured the museum, I was aghast at the number and range of the exhibits, most of which was probably loot from India. There was a quantity of stuffed animals either hanging from the walls or standing stiffly on an artificial grassy bank, poised to pounce upon their prey. The eyes of the animals touched me even though I knew that they were made of glass, for they seem to possess an irresistible homesickness for their natural habitat. Next, we went into the dining hall whose grandiosity was meant to impress. There were rooms and more rooms, but the one that appealed to me most was a small breakfast room, also called the Tapestry Room.

When the tour was over, Mrs. Tenison suggested that I return to my room to dress for dinner. She added that it would be a black-tie affair. I mounted the stairs leading to my room in a daze. I lay down on the bed. Dress up for dinner? All I had in my overnight bag was a change of shirt, a blue sweater and underwear. The prospect of going down to dinner was daunting. Perhaps I could hide in one of the many rooms and no one would be able to find me. My choice would be to hide behind the Bengal tiger in the overstuffed museum.

Too late, there was a knock on the door.

"Come in!"

Bryan came in bearing a tall glass upon a silver tray.

"Your cocktail, sir."

"Thanks. Sorry to have given you such a run around."

"Not at all, sir."

"You are still stuck in the same groove, always sirring me!"

"Very well, s ..."

"Makes me uncomfortable, being called sir by someone older than me."

"How would you like me to address you, s ..."

"Call me by my name, Poh Seng. Back home I was so used to people sirring the white man. I am uncomfortable with the term, with all its connotations. It keeps subordinates in their proper place."

"As you wish, sir. I shall call you by your name."

We both laughed. I was thinking how stubbornly we cling onto old habits.

"Did you visit Malaya when you were in the army, Bryan?"

"Only for a few months. Couldn't get used to the climate, the heat and humidity. It's like living in a bowl of warm soup, thick and heavy. I was young and fit then and could have gotten used to it. We lived well. Had *amahs* and our own cook. I even thought of becoming a rubber planter. Positions were plentiful after the war, never mind the lack of experience. And the pay and living conditions were much better than what I could get back here. But my ageing parents were not well ... I must go now. The guests will be arriving soon."

"Hope we can have another chance to chat later. Meanwhile, I've a problem. I have nothing appropriate to wear to dinner. All I have is another clean shirt."

"If you don't mind, I can lend you my tux. Or else perhaps Robin's, if it is here. I'll go and check. Be back in a jiffy."

Bryan returned in a few minutes with a tuxedo draped over his arm.

"It might be too big, but try it on."

69

Alas, it was much too big for me. So there was nothing to be done except to brave through the dinner in just a shirt and trousers. After some discussion, Bryan loaned me a black polo-neck sweater. At least, I thought ruefully, it was black and the high collar would protect my neck at the table.

All too soon the dinner gong sounded and slowly I made my way downstairs. Bryan was waiting at the bottom and escorted me to the dining room. This was much smaller than the large banquet room we had visited earlier.

"Everyone's here, and punctual to the minute," Bryan whispered, steering me towards Mrs. Tenison, who was engaged in conversation with some of her guests. All the men were in dinner jackets, the ladies in finery. I could see they were upper crust, all right. Everyone exuded an air of self-composure. They wore such an enviable at-home-ness, an unquestionable sense of belonging, that an outsider is immediately singled out: anyone who's not born into this and doesn't belong. And why was I even there, in the first place? Mrs. Tenison had said that she was inviting me because her friends might find me interesting. Interesting? Like a dancing bear, perhaps? So, knowing all this, why did I consent, why did I come? When I knew full well that back home, we would never have sat down to sup at the same table. I felt very much an interloper and was seized by an uncomfortable self-consciousness. I stood out like a sore thumb, my clothes conspicuous, my demeanour downright rebellious like that of a colonial malcontent. I braced myself to run through a gauntlet of sneers and jeers but nothing of that sort happened. Instead I waded through a sea of smiles and warm friendship from everyone.

When I got to Mrs. Tenison, I offered my apologies for my inadequate dress. Truth was I did not even own a tux to my name, I confessed.

"It's unimportant, doesn't matter. It's only a dress code, a social convention. And I dare say a convention that perhaps is out of date. After all, we're living in more egalitarian times, thank goodness!"

"Hear! Hear!" The company agreed. Yet I wondered if the opinion was unanimous. Do we all stand for change? If so, there's hope that human beings can change for the better. But I wondered. It sounded so easy.

Our hostess took me around, introducing me to everyone. Instinctively, I remained guarded, but all the guests, without exception, were polite and friendly. At the beginning, we exchanged small talk, inconsequential pleasantries. For some reason, I felt and acted defiantly, with a fearless invincible glint in my eyes. I hoped that they would not trifle with me. For I was sensitive and averse to being laughed at.

We stood about, chatting, nursing the drinks in our hands. By the time we sat down to dinner, a general relaxation had settled on the company and outright laughter laced the hum of animated conversation. The table was a sparkling affair, sumptuous with elaborate plate settings and an array of highly polished silver, skilfully folded napkins, shiny candelabra with long, phallic candles, and luxuriant flower displays from the flower garden which still exuded scent in the night.

I had begun to enjoy myself and couldn't help but let down my guard. And I did this most willingly. For some moments, I looked at the scene before me as if I were a spectator, and had no active participation in the proceedings at all. I felt detached like some guardian angel hovering above the dinner party, keenly observing the event, but somehow myself invisible to others, floating benignly below the high ceiling.

"You must miss good Malayan food. What do you think of Irish cuisine?" asked Mrs. Forster, the Brigadier General's wife, seated to my left. Her name was Pansy, and she must have been a septuagenarian. Copious old-age freckles stained her bare arms, giving her a certain frailty. Mrs. Tenison had intimated to me earlier that she had been a fabulous beauty when young, her fame known through the length and breadth of India. I was unable to find the striking beauty hidden by the devastations of time. I felt a touch of poignancy as I turned to speak to her.

"O yes! I miss home cooking very much, and spicy food. I can't live without chillies. My family has to send supplies of chillies every few months. Otherwise, I won't know what to do."

"I know just what you mean. We've lived so long in India, grown accustomed to the food and everything. We have great difficulties whenever we travel."

Brigadier General Forster chimed in, "My wife's absolutely right. It's a disgrace that there isn't a single Indian restaurant in Dublin."

Mrs. Forster added, "One has to go all the way to London. By the way, we've been to Malaya and we love the people and the wonderful food. Especially from the hawker stalls."

"Are you at Trinity?" Mrs. Sinclair asked. A tall, thin woman with expressive hands with which she sketched the air theatrically as she talked. She was married to Ian Sinclair, the pastor of the Anglican Church in the village.

"No, I'm at UCD."

Pastor Sinclair was physically the opposite of his wife. A fat man with a deep tan, a self-professed sun-worshipper, a surprising trait for a person of his calling.

"We attended the weirdest play recently in Dublin. At the small theatre in Trinity, didn't we, my dear?" the man of God said to his wife. Frequently at dinner that night, one of them would begin a conversation and pass the other half of it to the spouse to continue. The direction of this truncated conversation could be reversed. Really skilful and impressive teamwork. They must be long married to perform this tandem act. Such deftness could only come from long and arduous practice.

"Yes," Mrs. Sinclair continued. "It was a sort of premier of a new play. A new play called 'End of the Game'. A certain Mr. Biscuit was the playwright."

I could not allow this mistake to stand and interjected, "Beckett! It's probably *Endgame* by Samuel Beckett. The same spelling as the Beckett who was assassinated at Salisbury Cathedral!"

Too late, I realized that I sounded like a show-off. My face coloured. Goes to show what a novice I was in polite society.

"And you were saying something about the play?" our good hostess interceded, steering us all to safer ground.

"As I was saying," the pastor continued, "it really was a strange play. One of those avant-garde affairs. Throughout the entire play, the two principle characters were stuck in garbage bins. Another was dumped onto an armchair and the fourth actor shuffled around like an idiot."

Mrs. Sinclair took over, "And the strange thing was that the audience were laughing their heads off. At what, escapes me. Isn't that so, dear?"

"That is so, my dear. I may not be the most intelligent man around, but at least I could infer that it was taking place in a derelict land after nuclear bombs had smashed the rest of the world to smithereens. But I do agree, I didn't find it funny. It's as if my parishioners were laughing as I gave a fire and brimstone sermon."

I was about to make a comment, but thought better of it.

The Honourable Oliver Goodness turned to me and asked, "Tell me, are you fond of music?" He was well known as the heir to a big brewery conglomerate and a British Peer.

"I've just begun listening to music. I have much to learn."

"Do you know the folk music in your country?"

"I'm afraid I am totally ignorant. You see, we were never taught music at school except for some English songs, but I am confident that there are students now studying music who will research this one day."

"Excellent! It's very important. I would like to invite you to one of the Sunday musical afternoons at my home. You should be able to hear some old traditional music. It's very informal, just come as you are."

A simple man, who would be happier in country tweed than a tuxedo, I conjectured.

Ruth Tenison brought the conversation around to a discussion of the Merdeka or Freedom talks then taking place in London. A smart hostess' ploy. She wanted to know what I thought of the talks between the UK and the Malayan government then taking place in the British capital.

"From what I hear, they are not going too well. Her Majesty's government plays the recalcitrant, stubbornly trying to hold on to the dwindling empire."

"That's just not so!" the Conservative MP from Essex interjected. This was Gordon Sutcliff, a third-term Tory MP He had come alone. "It's the Malayans who are being unreasonable, and short-sighted. They are unwilling to see that only the British can come between the various factions with their physical presence. If I may be permitted to speak frankly, we are concerned about the racial problems and the political realities. The rivalries are too wide and entrenched for anyone to ignore. We fear the real potentiality of a ghastly catastrophe. We must act responsibly. We have to be resolute in these matters."

"That's pure exaggeration. Pure presumption, Mr. Sutcliff. The problem is the British really want to stay on and enjoy the benefits they have been used to."

"My opinion," offered the Brigadier General, "is to clear all problems with a strong hand. General Templar's now in charge. Give him time and he'll settle the situation in the proper manner. After the murder of Sir Henry Gurney, the British did the right thing in despatching Templar. He has a firm hand."

"That's nonsense! What Templar's doing to my country is to herd our poor farmers into so-called security villages where freedom of movement has been curtailed. They're just concentration camps surrounded with barbed-wire fences' and armed guards. It's an offence against humanity."

During the last couple of years, I had begun to take an interest in politics, especially that of Southeast Asia. This was my homeground and what happened to the region affected Malaya directly. It was a heady period marked by nationalism and the rising tide of the struggle for freedom, as seen by the whole of Indochina. There was an edginess and heightened nervous tension in the air. The public was politicized, and not surprisingly, my own generation as well. Students' union s and associations sprouted up everywhere, including Dublin, albeit a backwater compared to London. I had become very involved and had been elected the Honorary Secretary General in my second year at university, organising student functions from dances to cultural shows to debates and talks. I had become a student leader! I could now stand up to the Tory MP of Essex at Mrs. Tenison's dining table. Indeed I was eager for the fray.

The topic was hotly argued over the table, dominated by the MP and myself. My subscriptions to the *Manchester Guardian* and the *New Nation* were paying off. My Sunday ritual of reading *The Observer* from cover to cover ensured my being abreast of current events.

When dinner was over, we adjourned to the drawing room for coffee and more drinks. Bryan was kept on his toes. The evening had been a success and Mrs. Tenison was delighted. The conversation had been lively and entertaining, and no one had been ignored. Everyone had been drawn in. And I, like everyone else, had enjoyed myself thoroughly.

Later, we stood in the entrance hall, saying our good-byes. The Brigadier General and his wife were the first to leave. When we were alone, Mrs. Tenison told me that the Brigadier General had retired four or five years ago. They seemed a bit lost, forlorn. The army had been their home and family and they floundered away from it. The Brigadier General had had a fairly distinguished career and spent a good deal of it in India. The Forsters had no children.

Mr. Gordon Sutcliff shook my hand firmly and warmly. It denoted he wanted no lingering hostility between us and a possible friendship.

"My congratulations! You gave a good performance," as though he was talking about politics as a form of theatre.

"Any thought of playing an active role in politics, in public affairs?"

"Yes," I lied.

"Excellent! I am pleased to hear that. Too many educated fellows with your background eschew this dirty business called politics, and are only swayed by money. Your country needs you and I would only advise that you be diligent in your studies in England, learn as much from us of all that's best. We can keep on maintaining a close tie between us that could be of value for our two countries. This is the mandate enshrined in the British Commonwealth."

I said, "But I am studying in Ireland!"

"I stand corrected. Anyway, all the best. Call me up when you're in London, and I'll show you the House and its operations."

Then he was gone.

Mrs. Tenison told me later that Mr. Sutcliff was really a decent chap. It would be worthwhile having him as a friend. He was considered an up and rising MP. Already, he sat on two important Parliamentary committees.

Next to exit was the pastor and his partner. "Well, young man. Goodnight to you, and all the best in your studies," he said, trying to sound fatherly.

The last to bid us goodnight was the Honourable Oliver Goodness. His hand, when I shook it, was warm and soft. "I will be glad to meet you again."

"Dear, dear Oliver," Mrs. Tenison appraised. "Ollie certainly lives up to his surname. He's a dear, and has the kindest of hearts. Unusual in the truly wealthy."

The evening was finally over. I thanked my hostess, went straight to bed, and floated effortlessly into sleep.

The next morning, farm fresh, I went to join Ruth, as she had insisted I called her, for breakfast in the lovely Tapestry

Room. The table was laid for two. Ruth enquired when my train was leaving for Dublin.

"At 3.20."

"Oh dear. It will be too early for my show."

"Show?"

"I was going to show you how I work my dogs. I work dogs for a living. Train them for hunters. Specifically Labrador Retrievers. I charge good money for this. The owners bring me their dog or dogs when they are under a year old for the programme of training. They are taught obedience, to follow their masters, as well as all sorts of other skills necessary to a hunting dog, such as ferreting, pointing, and retrieving. They are trained to bring back the downed booty, on whatever terrain, back to their master. A good hunting dog is very valuable. I used to go in for studding. The dogs that I handled were pedigree dogs of course. Don't do it now. Too much work."

"But why do you do all this?"

"First of all, for the money of course. Just because I live in a big house, doesn't mean I don't have to make a living. And I love the work. So I have the best situation, doing something I enjoy. Am I not fortunate?"

"You are a remarkable lady, that's what you are!"

"And I was going to show off with my dogs. You see, sometimes I like to play with them. For instance, I can get them to stand in a line with an interval of space in between each one. Then I get the dog in the first position to jump over the next dog, and so on. It's like a circus show. Children simply love it. I like to demonstrate how intelligent dogs are. Indeed, all animals are. People just don't appreciate this."

She then said there was something else she wanted to show me. I followed her down the long corridor towards the east wing at the back of the house. We walked through a large courtyard ringed with potted plants. It was very tranquil. We finally entered a room which was a study cum studio, cosy and comfortable and yet the whole effect contained a certain professionalism.

"This is where I write and illustrate children's books. I have my own publishing firm to produce them but I farm out the distribution to someone in Dublin. That's why I go down to Dublin so often, every third week or so. Most times, Bryan runs me down in the Bentley, though I often drive myself in the humble Rover."

I looked through some of her books and was very impressed. I was about to say something when she continued, "Don't ask me why I do this. I am not ashamed to work for my living. I intend to support myself if I can do so and not use my children's inheritance from their father. I think, after my husband's death, my work has kept me alive and happy. Yes, I am happy to be as involved as I am. I am not boasting, but there are other responsibilities and chores I have to bear. It's part of our station in life you see, of service to the community with whom we live. And you can always manage, even though you have 'no time'. We'll take a detour so that I can show you something else — like show and tell."

And so I came across the real treasure of Loughbawn. A small cottage set in perfect isolation in the very bower of nature.

"You may come and stay when the cottage is not occupied. For a few weeks if you like. You will not be disturbed. Sometimes we have guests to stay over, especially friends of my children. Anyway, you can use it to write your poetry."

So that was how I became a renowned dreamer, a man who is accused of being an escapist. My dreaming and love for cottages, huts, sheds and cabins became a lifelong love affair.

I went up several times to Loughbawn, to visit my dear friend, Ruth. I stayed in the cottage by myself, with my books and my portable typewriter. Sometimes, I had Ruth for company, which I always appreciated. And sometimes I saw her when she came to Dublin on business, which she made meaningful and rewarding in itself. She is a person for whom I have utmost regard and affection.

Chez Tenison. I attended parties there, with her family and friends. I recall one occasion, when Robin was there with his fiancée and some of their good friends, and the sheer fun and joy we had that charming weekend. We lay on the grass, consuming cakes and fresh strawberries and cream and drinking sparkling ice-cold champagne while listening to a recording of "My Fair Lady" which was currently playing in London.

I must confess I often denigrate the rich for all the standard reasons, but, having glimpsed a little of the happy life of Ruth Tenison, I am forever nostalgic.

The Reinvented Man

THE FBI AND THE CIA did it in the movies. And for all intents and purposes, are still at it in real life, causing people to disappear and then reappear elsewhere, furnished with a new name and other documents which are necessary for a person to function nowadays in society; such as a passport, an identity card, a driving licence, etc., etc. So much so, a man requires more credentials, assorted licences and permits than does a dog. To return to the point, a man, in other words, can be moved elsewhere, rather as one transplants a tree to another site.

Consider the case of my friend, Tom Pierre. Not because he had anything to do with the FBI, or the CIA, at least not to my knowledge, but he was constantly being made-over, groomed to keep pace with the demands of our changing lives. I have always thought of Tom Pierre as an example of the reinvented man.

As far as I know, Tom Pierre was born to a lower-class black family on the island of Trinidad. Everything about his past is misty and unclear, drawn from hints and imprecise information supplied by Tom Pierre himself. Which ought to be suspect, for he meticulously guarded his secrets, of which there were many. Mystery was his persona. Even his inconsistencies were deliberate. One could form the opinion that Tom Pierre was a liar, at which he would flash an ingenious smile, implying that it was a fair judgement and that he would not disagree with this verdict himself. As if being labelled a liar were an encomium and not an insult. I rather suspect he relished our puzzlement.

For a start, even Tom Pierre's surname was equivocal, and he possessed two of them. He could be, by his own reckoning, Thomas Christopher-Pierre one day, and Thomas Gyton-Pierre the following. They were both hyphenated, as you may have noticed. Now I don't know about you, but I have always regarded a hyphenated surname with awe, as if one was before a great personage. One feels impelled to bow or curtsey. And Tom Pierre would accept such tribute with natural born and bred graciousness.

On so-called Gyton-Pierre days, Tom Pierre readily furnished details of his paternal great-grandfather. Fernand Gaetane Pierre was the scion of a minor patrician family from Angoulême, in the west of France. He inherited a modest fortune, and on the demise of his father sailed to the West Indies. There he earned a reputation as a local Lothario, forming numerous liaisons with women of all colours. Tom Pierre's great-grandmother, a black beauty from the Royal House of Benin, was his favourite amour.

In time, the family name of Fernand Gaetane Pierre evolved to Gyton-Pierre.

On Christopher-Pierre days, his paternal great-grandfather was the second son of an English peer, who chose to try his luck in the Caribbean. Christopher Pare was a born adventurer and gambler who amassed a fortune from a spectacular winning streak at cards. He fell in love with an exquisitely beautiful siren from St. Lucia who became Tom Pierre's great-grandmother.

The name Christopher Pare evolved with time into the family name Christopher-Pierre.

One day, I was out to lunch with Richard Adeney at Soho in London. Richard was then the principal flautist with the London Philharmonic Orchestra, and had become a dear and close friend after I met him through Tom Pierre. Richard told me that he'd just visited Tom Pierre at Notting Hill Gate, and met, for the first time, Tom Pierre's mother! She was a big black woman, exuberant in manner and garb, and loquacious as a meat vendor at Brixton market. Her diction was quintessential Trinidadian. With her was a genial fellow countryman named Adam, a rough and tough man with a pacific manner. The point was, and here Richard shook his head in bewilderment, he couldn't tell if Adam was Tom Pierre's natural father or brother.

From what I have managed to sketch about Tom Pierre so far, it is fair to say that I believe that everything about him was suspiciously false and a transparent tissue of lies, but his friends overlooked this because of his great charm. I cannot say that I too had not fallen for his charm; he was an intriguing and likeable fellow. It's as if I was on his side. And most unabashedly, I was, and am.

For we were all liars, the whole bunch of us foreign students studying in Dublin in the 1950s. Let me elucidate. All of us were desperately alone and lonely, often both, if truth be told. We were mainly colonials adrift in the West. We'd come from homes where the white man was master, the big boss. An inferiority complex was something we were familiar with, and generally low self esteem. We were afraid of being laughed at, of being ridiculed, and so we lied. We spun lies about our backgrounds and our families, who were invariably illustrious and wealthy. Coloured students were the most vulnerable victims of this affliction, but white students were not immune.

There was a fellow by the name of Claude de Vere Browne from Mauritius, a complete nincompoop, whom I unaccountably liked. He had no redeeming features, I think, yet I befriended him and we often chatted over a cup of cappuccino at the Coffee Inn, the hub of my social world then. Or else we would go swimming and sunbathing at the Hole in the Wall at Malahide in the summer. And there, while reclining on towels to tan ourselves an imagined burnt-gold like youthful Hellenic Gods, all the while watching the heavenly girls go by, we would exchange anecdotes about those good old days back home, in Malaya or Mauritius, when slaves were slaves and masters rode magnificently on their steeds. Come to think of it, Claude rode at a riding school in Ballsbridge, Dublin, near the Horse Show Grounds. He would sometimes come into town in his jodhpurs, riding crop in hand. I must admit that he looked very handsome, his features like those of the male models in women's magazines, a rustic human animal, if there is such a term. As for me, I could hardly contain my envy. The pathetic cheapskate in me wanted to look like a male model too, a sexy animal wearing an aquamarine silk shirt with the top three buttons undone to show off my pecs. I was so enticed by this image that I actually went with Claude to enrol at the riding school. I paid good money for this folly.

The trainer was a wiry woman in her mid-thirties. She had dirty blond hair cut short like a boy and wore no make-up. We took an instant dislike to each other. Sabres drawn on first sight, she scrutinized me and said that I was inadequately dressed. I had on jeans and a yellow T-shirt.

"We're not operating a school for cowboys," she remarked.

She told me to mount a chestnut, a big horse named Cleopatra. Astride, I could feel its bulk move beneath me. I felt precarious. It was like sitting on a live and dangerous volcano.

The horse walked slowly round the enclosure. This was easy as pie, and after two rounds, I thought I could do this with my eyes closed.

"Good, jolly good. Now try a simple jump."

"I'm not so sure … What do I do?"

"Cleo'll do all the work. All you have to do is hang on. Watch it, here she goes!"

All I could feel was fear and panic, as Cleo seemed to have gone berserk, galloping towards an obstacle directly in our path. I got ready for the jump. Just as I was expecting to fly over like Pegasus, Cleo suddenly applied the brakes. It was I who flew, making a flip in the air. I landed an untidy mess on the grass, knocking my head hard on the ground.

Crack! I saw stars. That put paid to my ambition to membership of the mystic riding club.

Claude's father was an Englishman who went to Mauritius after the war and joined the police force. Superintendent Browne married a local woman of French extraction, but not from one of the seven illustrious families. Claude was such a prig that he looked down on his mother, but revered his father, a macho hunk in uniform. He felt that his mother was a hindrance to his father's advancement in the colonial police force. How the bastard regaled me with his father's mistreatment of his prisoners, especially those sentenced to corporal punishment.

My own edifying contribution to this trashy conversation was to relate how it was a tradition in our (*ahem*) illustrious family for the first-born son to be carried about by servants, in their arms or in an ornate gold palanquin, so that my feet would not touch the base earth until I had attained the age of three years! Claude's eyes widened. He was hard put to top this!

At that time, I was sharing a flat with three other students from Malaya. It was not a bad deal but despite the comfort and its location near University College, Dublin, I found the environment boring and dull. I felt myself sinking into the doldrums, became easily irritable and found fault with everything and with every one of my flatmates. They were actually glad when I informed them I was contemplating shifting out.

Then I remembered how friendly they had been to me when I first came to Dublin and their attempts to make me feel at home.

It was some time before I began to feel better and made a kinder appraisal of myself. I was undergoing change, which I truly wanted, and I must go where I could effect this change. It was the very core of my life's adventure. I wanted to take whatever risks were necessary, for the alternative was to be passive and cautious, to be tied down and forsake the adventures that beckoned. Like a young bird, I wanted to sprout wings and take to the sky. Look! I'm growing new plumage, which will enable me to soar! O look! I'm already flying!

Then one night, I was invited to a party by some West Indian friends. The West Indians stood out at university because of their colour, physique and laughter. They seemed to laugh all the time. I was curious about them.

The party at Leeson Street was crowded and noisy when we arrived with the customary six bottles of Guinness. It took some effort to get up the stairs to the main room where the heart of the party pulsated. Here, a steel band was playing Calypso music and everyone was dancing. I had never seen such uninhibited joy, such a display of happiness. The dancers gyrated and jumped to the irresistible beat of the music. Everywhere I turned, I saw a celebration of life, saw faces beaming with smiles. These happy people were really the true sons and daughters of the sun! I was overwhelmed.

I wanted to be a West Indian. Yes! Even if I had to re-invent myself as one!

I began to hang around with my West Indian friends, gradually, imperceptibly absorbing some of their traits and behaviour. I cultivated a certain twang and bounce in my speech with frequent utterances of "O mon!" instead of "O man!", finding the former more fraternal.

I longed to look like them, envied them for their names. There was Courtney Bartholomew, a tall, statuesque and courtly young man, one of the top students, who always had a beautiful chick on his arm. Then there was Christopher Lloyd, shy and soft-spoken, who moved with the grace of a star basketball player.

I noticed that my West Indian friends never shortened their names. Their complete, intact and sometimes hyphenated names lent them a certain dignity. Unlike Herbert Hynes from the USA whose name had been shortened to Herb or Herbie. Herb claimed to be the nephew of Louis "Satchmo" Armstrong. Sure he was, we teased, and Bartholomew's the cousin of Duke Ellington! A year later, Satchmo gave a concert in Dublin, much to our joy. Courtney Bartholomew accompanied Herb to the great jazzman's dressing room and witnessed him hugging his nephew. Satchmo was indeed Herb's uncle!

I hung out with the West Indian gang for many months, enjoying their parties, following them to cricket matches, but slowly the shine faded. It was like having a surfeit of good things; you lose your appetite when you're too full. Yes, perhaps that was what I went through, losing my enthusiasm for that constant yen for happiness, as if life was one joyous party.

But enough! Let's get back to Tom Pierre.

I actually heard Tom Pierre before I met him. It was at a party thrown by the Honourable Oliver Goodness, who cultivated artists and intellectuals. Many of his guests were from the social register. I was quaffing drinks as fast as I could while desperately searching for a familiar face when I heard a cultivated Oxbridge accent discoursing wittily on Léopold Senghor's theory of negritude. A black, black man with skin a moonless, midnight black, glorious and glittering, was holding court in the midst of a group of admiring listeners. He was handsome to boot. Move over Sidney Poitier!

I recognized him as a fellow medical student at University College. In the weeks that followed, Tom Pierre and I began meeting at the Coffee Inn and Davy Byrne's. We made an odd pair: I in my grey gabardine coat bought from Cecil Gees while Tom Pierre always cut a suave figure in an impeccable suit complete with waistcoat. Tucked into the little pocket near the left lapel would be a small silk handkerchief which looked as though it was pushed in carelessly, although in actual practice it took a great deal of arranging to attain that casual look. An umbrella was another accessory to this ensemble. Tom Pierre twirled the slimmest, meanest black brolly like a walking stick, with style and insouciance.

He was my first homosexual friend. At that time, I was still ignorant about sex, having little experience. Those days, homosexuality was not so openly accepted. There was a great deal of ignorance, which led to prejudice and persecution. It was a criminal act and its practitioners could be thrown in jail. And in Catholic Ireland, it was a mortal sin. Many became closet, or secret homosexuals. Their lives were, of necessity, somewhat clandestine. Not so with Tom Pierre. He was more blatant than most about his sexual preferences.

I must admit, I was a little uneasy and embarrassed when Tom Pierre first told me that he was a homosexual. The ignoramus that I was, I harboured fears for instance that homosexuality was contagious, like the flu or chicken pox!

One day, Tom Pierre asked if I would like to share a flat or house with him. At first this sounded suspiciously like a sexual proposition. Would I get sodomized one dark night?

I told him that I was a true blue heterosexual and that there was no use in anyone trying to convert me. He reassured me that he would not jump me. Then added he could not vouch for his friends as I was a sexy fellow.

Soon after, Tom Pierre told me about a house he had found. It was perfect in every way, including an affordable rent. A real find which we mustn't let slip.

And so we moved into No. 24 Pembroke Park.

During the ensuing weeks and months that Tom Pierre and I shared the house, not only did I have no regrets, but I count it truly as one of the most important periods in my life. My sharing with him was a positive learning experience. It influenced my life profoundly.

For instance, Tom Pierre would stand by the stairs landing and belt out, "Wake up! It's Sunday! The sky's clear and blue and we have a scrumptious breakfast. Bacon and eggs and toast which is being warmed in the oven to be enjoyed with dear Ruth Tenison's homemade strawberry jam!"

Is there a better way to be woken up, hitting the runway smoothly, soft and meticulous like a glider plane in the hands of an expert pilot slow-landing his craft? To re-enter the world thus, to rejoin one's life with such tender mercy? It is to breed optimism, that rare plant.

So to be ushered into the day by a sampling of Mozart, or Bach, such aural epiphanies, is to be blessed. Give us each day our daily breath, each hour also, and suffer us not into avoidance, but rather into engagement, every waking hour of our conscious life. For it is on Earth as it is in Heaven.

Living with Tom Pierre, dear God, is to return home after a long day, to find my bed strewn with plucked rose petals as a gift of friendship. Even on disastrous hangover mornings, when there seemed to be no good tidings or cheer, Tom Pierre would only mildly complain, "Kitchen's a big mess from last night's party. I'll clean up. Can't stand the mess. I'll lay out a simple lunch in the afternoon. Nothing fancy, I'm afraid. Anyhow, we're clean run out of provisions, our kitty's nearly empty. Naughty of you not to complete the shopping last week. Don't mean to nag. On second thoughts, I ought to really nag you. You're sometimes too, too much, you know that! Shall I put on Dennis Brain's Horn Concerto by Wolfgang? Blow out all the cobwebs in our brains! What say you?"

Soon afterwards, strains of the Horn Concerto filled the house, borne up as if by magic, an adequate miracle by itself. Music now admixed with domestic sounds from the kitchen, of cutting and slicing, pots and pans banging into each other with a syncopation worthy of jazz. I had just begun to be acquainted with jazz, and listening to Miles Davis trumpeting as Jeanne Moreau strolled that long take up to the scaffold brought responsive tears. It was all so EXQUISITE!

All this happening at No. 24 Pembroke Park on a serendipitous Sunday morning in the summer of '56.

One other component of our Sunday morning ritual was to nip down to the newsagent for the Sunday *Observer*, gripping the heavy tome safe under our armpits, anticipating the pleasure to come. We sat at our small kitchen table and shared the newspaper. We discussed the news and I settled down to reading my favourite columnists, Kenneth Tynan on Theatre and Penelope Mortimer on Cinema. Finally, the book and art reviews. A substantial feast, as we plugged into the world. Or, rather, to what was going on in London, the intellectual and cultural capital of our world.

To return to that particular Sunday, Tom Pierre had invited a couple of friends to tea at a picnic in our back garden, which he always referred to as "the orchard". Why not? After all, there were two apple trees and one pear tree. That afternoon, we sat or lay on a rug spread out on the grass. There were hot scones with Ruth Tenison's ubiquitous homemade strawberry jam and Ceylon tea, brewing in an elegant teapot that Tom Pierre had purchased from Portobello Road.

The gift of Tom Pierre to embellish an occasion or a chore into something significant and pleasurable, made living with him a delightful experience. He could turn a task into an occasion. Life then was filled with surprises as Tom Pierre went through a day or a week inventing or enhancing a simple mundane act into something special. He would celebrate a beautiful piece of music or a delicate tea cup with equal enthusiasm. This was his richness, not in wealth but the ability to savour the best in everything.

Thanks to his firm grasp on home management, we managed to live surprisingly well on our limited student allowances. We even hired a cleaning woman, a Mrs. O'Bryan who came in once a week to char. She was obviously enthralled with her foreign gentlemen and anxious to please, especially Tom Pierre, whom she revered.

Mrs. O'Bryan was a heaven-sent solution to our problem, which surfaced in the very first weeks of our sharing the house. Tom Pierre and I were very different people. He was neat and tidy, while I was untidy and disorderly. To Tom Pierre, everything had a proper place, while to me, any place was the proper place for everything. He said that my recalcitrant messiness was slothful. I countered that he was trying to control me.

But on the whole, I admired Tom's masterly application of the home budget and despite my complaints, I learnt much from him. We entertained often, inviting small numbers of good friends and interesting acquaintances to dinner. Tom Pierre did most of the planning and cooking as he was an excellent chef. His *boeuf bourguignon* and *coq au vin* were memorable. He was a true epicurean, often inventing new dishes, embellishing them with spices and herbs. When the guests arrived in the evening, our little house glowed with fresh flowers and candlelight and the smell of good cooking.

Those days in Dublin, there seemed to be a party almost every night. By closing time, everyone knew where the night's party was being held. Armed with bottles of stout or wine, the crowd continued their revelry at that night's venue. Most of these parties were nothing more than an extension of the pubs' closing hour and just a drinking binge. Tom Pierre then proposed that we hold a really good wild party once a fortnight with the mandate "To Enlighten Humanity and Celebrate Life!" To ensure that only desired guests were admitted, we persuaded two big chaps to act as bouncers. Tom Pierre or I would vet the newcomers. In this manner, our parties gained the stamp of exclusivity.

Once in a while, Tom Pierre would hold one of these parties exclusively for his homosexual friends. I agreed, provided that I could do likewise and hold a strictly heterosexual affair. Our parties were much talked about and our circle of friends grew. We were as pleased as kids.

Tom Pierre and I shared No. 24 Pembroke Park for two years, and broke up our arrangement the year he summered in the south of France. The following year was an intense and solemn one, as we braced ourselves for the final examination. It had taken six long years of hard work and perseverance. We were finally at the threshold. One afternoon, I took a short break from the medical library to enjoy a stroll at the Iveagh Gardens nearby. I met Tom Pierre. I asked him what his plans were after the examination. Without hesitation, he asserted that he was returning to Trinidad, where he intended to set up an exclusive medical clinic. He confided in me that he was going to import a Humber with a liveried chauffeur, a white man, of course. And a pair of spotted Dalmatians. And he would build a beautiful house.

I believed in Tom Pierre, and had no difficulty with all the things he intended to do. The only surprise was his returning to Trinidad. I imagined that it would be more difficult for him to live there than, say, London. This reinvented man would be conspicuous and vulnerable and I was concerned that he might find the society of the islanders intolerant. But I kept mum. He was old enough and skilful enough to negotiate his way through life. I did laugh, visualizing Tom Pierre sitting grandly in his chauffeured Humber, cruising the backwaters of Port of Spain. Accompanied by the two Dalmatians.

About ten years later, after our class had lost contact with one another, dispersing to all nooks and corners of this global world, I went to London from Singapore, where I was then living. I saw Richard Adeney and asked him about news of Tom Pierre. Richard informed me that he was hale and hearty, and in response to my queries, said, yes, Tom Pierre had built a beautiful house by the beach outside of the capital. Yes, he had a chauffeur and a pair of spotted Dalmatians. But he owned a silver Jaguar, not a Humber.

A few years later, I met up with Tom Pierre in London. He was his same self, suave and impeccably groomed. Like his Dalmatians.

Another ten years passed before I ran into Tom Pierre again, again in London. He did not look well. There was a certain shadow on his face, a drawn and dispirited man who seem to be looking for some missing thing in his life. I asked him, but he would not be drawn out. I let him be. It was Richard who divulged that he was having a bad affair with an impecunious young man, who, moreover, Richard suspected, was addicted to hard drugs. He was fearful that Tom Pierre might be driven to drugs himself. He was brokenhearted, and his lover gave him great pain.

It was another ten years later that I heard from Richard by long-distance telephone that Tom Pierre had just died from AIDs.

Falling in Love with Love

Falling in love with love is falling for make-believe
Falling in love with love is playing the fool ...
I fell in love with love, with love everlasting
But love fell out with me

I WAS HUMMING THAT CATCHY TUNE while riding my Lambretta through a moderate drizzle, under the usual grey, melancholic sky of Dublin, the kind of weather best described as nondescript or neither here nor there. Yet enough to induce a heart-yearning ache in a susceptible would-be poet. In other words, I was suffering from want of love. O if only I could fall in love, and be loved in turn, what magnificent poetry I could write! Alas, I could only sigh, more and more often these days, exasperated by a sense of un-lovedness that was unbecoming to a grown man, even more so for one who was poetic. What are poets made for, if not for love? I was 20 years old, Dublin was full of pretty girls and I had no one to love. O woe is me!

I recalled the words of Verlaine:

Il pleure dans mon coeur
Comme il pleut sur la ville;
Quelle est cette langueur
Qui pénètre mon coeur?

It rains in my heart
As it rains on the town;
What is this languor
Which skewers my heart?

The wet air stung my face. I turned up the collar of my raincoat. It hung in a shapeless mess on my body. I felt that my life was not getting anywhere. Yes, it rained in my heart.

Earlier that morning, Jean Robinson had called. She had just returned from London, where she was studying at RADA, the Royal Academy of Dramatic Arts. Jean and I had met a year ago at a party. I found her intelligent and interesting and we had talked most of that evening. After that first meeting, we began seeing each other quite often.

Jean was a true free spirit, ahead of her time. She did not wear makeup, her reason being "Because I am an actress. When I am acting, I enter into the role of the character I am playing. I attempt to assume her total personality: the way she looks, her gestures, her very soul. I find it easier to start off with a naked face. So no cosmetics for me."

She was a vegetarian at a time when being a vegetarian was unusual and rare. Fortunately, she was not the fanatical kind who disapproved when you ate a decent chop.

We were not romantically attached and there was an easiness about our friendship that was comfortable. Now and again when she was in Dublin, she would stay over at my place and we would talk far into the night. When she was away, she would send me the odd postcard. Once she sent me a postcard with a painting by Vlaminck, who was not well-known at the time. This was her way of championing the obscure. I was very fond of Jean.

We had agreed to meet at Bewleys. This was one of my favourite places in Dublin: a restaurant that glowed like a jewel from the light cast by the beautiful stained glass windows on its walls, and was filled with the sweet aromatic scent of rich coffee and tea and freshly baked bread and pastries. There one could sit alone and feel at ease, or have a quiet conversation with a close friend.

I spotted Jean seated at one of the wooden tables near the entrance. She was talking to a girl wearing a duffle coat even in the heat of summer.

Jean and I embraced and she introduced her friend.

"Hadley Rice and I were classmates in school. Her father's the Canadian Ambassador to Ireland."

We shook hands. Her hand was as small as a little girl's. Almost everything about her was diminutive, including her soft voice. I turned my attention to Jean. She was telling me that Hadley was a student at Trinity. She added that Hadley loved poetry.

"Did I tell you that Poh Seng recited the whole of Omar Khayyam to me one night? So you two have a lot in common. Poh Seng is a poet. He needs someone to listen to his verse and Hadley has a copious capacity to listen."

"Are you trying to match us, you wicked, wicked WOEMANN you?" I teased.

"Of course not! I dearly love this man, don't forget that, Hadley. I'm only lending him to you until my return."

"I never return anything I borrow. You're taking a big risk leaving Poh Seng with me," she countered.

We sat for a long time over coffee. Jean and I had a lot to talk about since we had not seen each other for some months. Hadley sat quietly listening to our animated banter. Then it was time to part. Hadley and I walked Jean to her bus stop. I had offered to take Hadley back to Dalkey on my Lambretta.

The drizzle had stopped and the sky was clear. Hadley put her arms around my waist. We rode in companionable silence, enjoying the fresh evening breeze. When we reached the heights overlooking the bay at Dalkey, a long stretch of beach crescented like a new moon, Hadley told me that the bay reminded her of the Bay of Naples. We headed down the sinuous bends towards the shore where the embassy was situated.

Just as we arrived, a Cadillac drove up. A small bald man in a white linen suit stepped out and a woman came out of the house to meet him. Hadley introduced me to her parents.

We stood on the porch making small talk.

"So you are a medical student ..." Mrs. Rice said.

"He's also a poet," Hadley interjected.

"How interesting. We are having a party to celebrate Canada Day next week. Would you like to come?"

I thanked them and took my leave.

❧

I had just moved to a flat in Rathmines which I shared with Steve Millan. Steve and I had met by chance.

A few weeks before, the B company of an opera from Milan had come to Dublin. I had never heard an Italian opera, so invested in a ticket to attend Puccini's *La Bohème*. Part of my education, I reasoned.

I decked myself up for the occasion in my best suit and even purchased a red carnation for my lapel. As soon as Mimi sang the first aria, I fell hopelessly in love with her. As the opera progressed, I was so overwhelmed by the music and by emotion that I was weeping uncontrollably. I wept pure tears, buckets of it as if the tear-making factory had gone berserk. The deluge flowed down my face, although I tried hard to wipe it away. My handkerchief was soaked through and I was forced to use the decorous little silk square from my lapel pocket.

I tried to cry stealthily, and when both kerchiefs were saturated, wiped my tears first on the left sleeve of my suit and then on the right sleeve. I dreaded the interval when the house lights would come on and expose me. At the end of the first act when the lights flooded the auditorium, I was trapped, caught in the act. Surreptitiously, I turned towards my neighbour sitting near the aisle. He was crying too, tears coursing down his face! We stared at each other, then began laughing uncontrollably.

"Man, I need a beer!" He introduced himself. "I am Steve Millan."

"I am Goh Poh Seng. Wasn't the opera fantastic? It's a first time experience for me."

"It's my first time too. It's truly overwhelming."

We went down to the bar together and after the interval, returned to our seats and wept copiously and happily through the rest of the opera.

Afterwards, we headed for the nearest bar together. It was near closing time and we just made it for the last drink. Steve then invited me home for a nightcap so we took the bus to Rathmines. He had half a bottle of rum, which was heaven-sent. We sat up all night talking. I learnt that Steve was looking for a flatmate. His fiancée, Brenda, had been forced to delay her trip from Trinidad and would not be joining him for another six months. I liked Steve and asked if I could share the flat until Brenda came. It would save me the onerous task of looking for a place and Steve from looking for a temporary tenant. So fate, or the Italian B opera company, took a hand. By the end of the week, I had moved into the small two-bedroom flat.

I have never met a man more in love than Steve Millan. He never stopped talking about Brenda. It was always Brenda this and Brenda that. The two of them were childhood sweethearts and had been going together since they left their prams. Steve was studying geology and always walked around with a hammer in his hand, tapping at rocks and stones. He was of mixed parentage, his skin the colour of *café au lait* but his eyes were a startling blue. He was good-natured and likeable and had many friends.

His father had been the manager of the West Indian subsidiary of an American movie distributor. In this position, he used to look after and entertain visiting movie stars to Trinidad. Steve was not averse to exploiting this situation.

"You shook hands with John Wayne! If it were me, I wouldn't wash my hands for a week, maybe forever."

And then, there were the movie posters, much sought-after collectibles. Steve would hand them out to his friends. He had a really happy childhood. By the age of 13, he had become Brenda Gonzalez's one and indisputable boyfriend.

Now he pined for his Brenda in the small flat in Rathmines, Dublin. I was amazed that a grown man could reach such a stage of extraordinary distress. It was just like the opera.

I envied him. My problem was I had no one to love. I was like a man with a disability, a man incomplete. I knew I must fall in love with someone. But who? That was the question.

I listed all the women I knew and liked. I could only think of three: Patsy O'Sullivan, Joan Trimble and Jean Robinson. Patsy and Joan were already happily married so I had enough sense to leave them alone. That left only Jean. I was fond of Jean, she was intelligent, witty and we had a lot in common. She was good company and great fun. But I had reservations. I was not attracted to her physically. So that was that. What could I say? There was no one. What a dismal thought. Had I overlooked anyone? Perhaps someone I just met. O yes, there was Hadley Rice.

A few days later, I received a formal invitation from the Canadian Embassy to the Canada Day celebrations. I threw it on my desk. By the time I decided to go, the date for the RSVP was over. Nevertheless, I went to the reception. Apart from the Rices, I did not know anyone there. I focused on the food till Hadley came to the rescue.

"I am so glad you came," she said.

I was glad to see her too.

"This is boring, I'm afraid. If you like, we could take a stroll by the beach."

"OK. Let's do that."

We crossed the street to the beach. The black sheen in the water extended as far as the eye could see. There was something bewitching in that late summer evening. We walked for awhile in companionable silence.

"Have you read *The Outsider*?" she asked.

"Camus? Yes I have."

"No, Colin Wilson."

"No, I've not done so. I know he's all the rage in London these days. Have you read him?"

"Yes, I have. As a matter of fact, I'm reading him a second time," she declared.

I studied her face. So young, yet there was a certain gravity which I found appealing.

"Myself," I said, "I am drawn to Camus' Meursault. I feel a certain affinity with him."

"He's so negative!"

"Exactly! It's the negativity I find intriguing. Daily we are confronted with the futility and meaninglessness of human existence."

"I'm sure you don't believe that. You can't be like that. It just doesn't square if you are studying medicine."

"You're right. It doesn't square. This is what I am grappling with. I seem to have lost my enthusiasm for medicine. I am contemplating giving it up." I had been having these thoughts of late. I was only surprised that I was talking about it.

"You must be kidding. No one gives up medicine so easily," she commented.

"It isn't easy. I have gone this far. The impact it would have on my family. It would be devastating. They have pinned such hopes on me."

"It's a very grave decision. You must think about it carefully."

"You're being presumptuous, Hadley."

"Oh I'm sorry," she cried, her cheeks colouring.

"Don't be sorry. We should always speak the truth to each other if we can be close friends. Would you like that Hadley?"

She nodded shyly.

And I shall make her my little captive audience!

We continued to walk slowly along the beach. With my encouragement, she talked about Wilson's book. She did it well. Who knows, perhaps I would be her captive audience. I told her I was working on a book of poems.

"I would like to read it, if you will let me have the manuscript."

"It's still in the early stages. Needs a lot more time and labour. I'll let you read it when it's ready."

"I don't mind if they are not quite finished. I can understand that a poet would only show work that he's confident about. But it would be good if the poet has someone who can be a kind of sounding board, or maybe just a sympathetic reader."

"How uncanny, I was just thinking the same thing!" I said. Ideally, this person would be a soulmate, completely trustworthy, to whom I could lay bare my most profound secrets and receive understanding. That very moment, I felt myself tottering on the edge of love. What a surprise! What a fitting development. We walked on for awhile and then Hadley said she must return to the party. After all, she was a host.

Later, I zoomed away on my Lambretta, a shining knight in armor, riding my steed, the night a magical entity wrapping around me with its mantle of stars, while a celestial choir sang out to the vast and conspiring universe: LOVE LOVE LOVE. So it was revealed, love was so easy to find!

That weekend, I invited Hadley to see *La Bohème*. Steve Millan was so ecstatic that I had fallen in love at last that he raided the gas meter box. He left a note:

> Dear Mr. Meterman, I'm borrowing two pounds, ten shillings for an emergency affair in the realm of love. We need to buy some gin to celebrate. Will repay in due course. Thanks. Yours sincerely, Steve Millan.

The crowd at the Gaiety Theatre that night was all dressed up for the occasion as though ready to enter another world, the world of music and love. Then I saw Hadley approaching. She was simply dressed, but had used lipstick and light make-up, responding in her own way to the occasion. I was glad. Wanted this to be a special evening. We entered and took our seats. I wanted to, but did not, hold her hand. Rudolfo sang,

> *Your tiny hand is frozen,*
> *Let me warm it into life ...*

and the damn tears started brimming again. They flowed without constraint. I loved every minute of it. As the wonderful music of Puccini gushed over me, I felt full of love for everything in the universe, especially Hadley, seated sedately but dry-eyed beside me. How she could sit thus without crying a bathtub load, I don't know. A discordant note dampened me momentarily. Then the magic of the music took hold of me again. I was under a spell. It was as if there was some sweet static in the atmosphere surrounding the two of us.

Afterwards, we wandered through the streets of Dublin on that bewitching night, and yes, I did take her tiny hand in mine.

ᐁ❧

From then on, we began to see each other frequently. We would meet after classes and stroll along the streets and parks of Dublin. Sometimes we would browse in the bookshops on College Green or sit over coffee at Bewleys and the Coffee Inn.

Ours was a pure and poetic love affair. Whenever we were together, we held hands self-consciously but that was as far as it went. We never even kissed. It was frustrating, being always on the fringe, with no promise of anything more. It was like unripe fruit, a green papaya which gave off neither soft sweet nourishment nor inviting scent. When I was not with her, I wrote her long impassioned letters. Some days, I would write to her as soon as I had returned home after one of our outings. I wrote about myself, my feelings and what I believed was happening to me. It was as if I had tapped an underground spring whose flow could not be stopped. Once I wrote: "You taught me to see beauty in an orange peel lying in the gutter." I felt this imagery was so profound that she could not fail to be dazzled. One weekend I wrote her a letter 100 pages long.

Her family began to be concerned. Her mother talked to Hadley about the unsuitability of our friendship. There were too many significant differences between us that could not be dismissed. I told Hadley that her mother was a discriminating, social-climbing old battle axe.

My own behaviour was peculiar. I didn't know what I wanted. I knew I wanted to be in love. I loved the throes of being in love.

One night, we attended a gala ball to celebrate Hari Raya, the Malay New Year. It was a grand affair held at the Shelbourne Hotel, one of the poshest venues in Dublin at the time. The gala was also graced by the Mayor of Dublin. I was strangely elated. I ate and drank and danced and sang and shouted. I got properly drunk. Or, rather, improperly drunk. I passed out and woke up the next morning on the cold marble floor of the Gents. I did not know whether it was night or day. There was a pervading odour of urine and disinfectant. I felt terrible.

That evening, I telephoned Hadley and was told she was not in. I rang several times the next day and could not get hold of her. I continued calling that whole week to no avail. I wrote several letters apologizing for my behaviour. She did not reply. It seemed that she did not want to have anything to do with me. I decided to ride over to Dalkey to apologize in person and was told she was not in.

I could not believe Hadley did not want to see me. I suspected her mother of holding her incommunicado. I decided to confront the dragon lady. I phoned the Residence and asked for Mrs. Rice. When she recognized my voice, she sternly asked what it was I wanted. I asked to speak to Hadley.

"It's simply out of the question, it's impossible," she stated. "You must leave her alone. There's no future in this relationship for Hadley. We come from different worlds. Moreover, she does not wish to speak to you."

"That can't be true!"

"It's the truth, trust me."

"No, Mrs. Rice, I don't trust you!"

The phone call was abruptly terminated.

The next few weeks, I was left high and dry. I could not concentrate on my studies. Life was bitter, no longer mingled with sweetness.

Then one winter night, the sky black like charcoal, I received a phone call from Jean Robinson. She had just returned from London. I felt buoyed just hearing her voice. We agreed to meet at Bewleys.

"You look well," I said greeting her with a hug.

"And you look terrible! What's happening to you?"

"I'm in love."

"With Hadley?"

I nodded. For some reason, I found it easy to talk to Jean about the affair. She listened sympathetically.

"What can I say? You and Hadley are close to me. I know you both well. It's hard to say this, but you are unsuited for each other."

"Why? Because we're of different races?"

"Of course I don't think that way. It has more to do with different backgrounds and personalities. In many ways, you two don't match. Before long, there will be serious conflicts."

"I know we have our differences, but two people in love can surpass them. There need not be complete compatibility, surely."

"It matters in your case and in Hadley's too. I want to be objective. But my gut feelings are that it will come to a bad end. I don't want it to happen to either of you."

"I understand your fears but they are unfounded." I was getting a little irritated by her negativity.

"And besides," she said, churning along the same track, "Hadley's only 19, and a very sheltered 19. I fear for her vulnerability."

"You fear, you fear, you fear too much, in my reckoning. I have no intention of hurting her. I'm not a monster. Whose side are you on, really?"

"Neither side. If anything, I'm on the side of common sense."

"And when did common sense have anything to do with love?"

We both laughed, our mutual irritation dissipated. We ordered lunch and she told me about the months she had spent in London. Then over coffee, Jean said:

"There's something I'm debating whether to tell you."

"Shoot!"

"I've given them my word that I won't tell you. If they find out, I'm in hot soup."

"C'mon! C'mon! Out with it."

"They've sent her away. Out of Dublin."

"They're crazy! To do that! Christ, can they do that in this day and age?"

"Yes, I was shocked. They must dislike you a lot."

"To Hell with them. I must find Hadley, must go to her. Jean, you must help me, get me her address."

Jean had visited the Residence on her return to Dublin. She was appalled when she learnt Hadley had left Trinity, where she was happy and doing well. She found out that Hadley was in Aix-en-Provence, staying with family friends. Jean had requested Hadley's address so that she could write to her. The parents had acquiesced, but only after Jean swore to keep it secret and only for her own use.

"So you see, darling, how far I would go on your behalf!"

"I knew that I could rely on you. You're such a special friend. You're an angel!"

I wrote to Hadley, not expecting any reply. For days I lived in suspension. Then her letter arrived.

She wrote that she was hurt and shocked by her parents' actions. It appeared they would take any measure to prevent her from seeing me. She was lonely and sad and missed Dublin. No, she had not forgiven me completely. I was so nasty to leave her alone at the Shelbourne. She signed off: "Yours, Hadley".

I read and reread her letter many times, hoping for some sign of her feelings for me. The only evidence was the word "Yours" at the end of the letter. There it is! I pressed the letter to my bosom.

I wrote to her straightaway, declaring my undying love. I received a reply scrawled large over the page:

"Yip Yip Yip I love you Hooray Yip Yip Hooray!"

The sky that morning was blue suddenly. I was seized with the mad idea of going to Aix-en-Provence to be with her. I was convinced I must go. I swallowed my pride, and went around my friends soliciting for loans. I managed to raise enough for the trip to Aix.

∽❧

The journey was long and arduous. I had to cross both the Irish Sea and the English Channel by ferry, and then there was the long train ride from Liverpool to Dover. The train ride in France was uneventful, much of the landscape wrapped in mist. My ticket did not entitle me to a bunk and I slept fitfully curled up on my seat foetal fashion. It was a marathon trip, but I was eager to be with my love.

Finally, early in the morning, I was unloaded onto the platform of a small country station. There were only a few people about. I showed them Hadley's address and one of them directed me to a small grey house. It was still dark and there was no one about. I knocked on the door. It was sometime before it was answered. An old woman stood there with an angry scowl on her face.

"Bonjour Madame. Mademoiselle Rice, est-elle à la maison?"

She uttered something in French that was beyond me. I just repeated *"Mademoiselle Rice? Mademoiselle Rice?"* until she understood. She then seized my arm and pointed at my wristwatch. It read 5.18! No wonder the poor woman was annoyed.

"Pardonnez-moi, pardonnez-moi!" I apologized, *"après ... après ..."* I gestured, hoping she would understand that I would return later, as I backed away. She nodded and shut the door.

I picked up my bag and walked towards the town centre. The sky was beginning to pale. I felt a hollowness in my stomach and started to look for a place where I could eat. I walked until I came to a small square. Two men were sweeping the front of a café. I asked in my best bazaar and rather bizarre French if I could have something to eat. One of them nodded and gestured to a table.

While he served me a croissant and hot chocolate, we began to converse in a mixture of English and French accompanied by a lot of gestures, laughing good-naturedly at our mutual awkwardness. Maurice was curious as to why I was in Aix-en-Provence. When I told him my story, he was indignant and cried, "Have courage! *L'amour* victor in the end, *mon ami!"*

Soon customers began drifting in. Maurice related my plight to all of them and they smiled at me and gestured encouragement.

I was getting sleepy and exhausted.

Maurice noticed this and asked if I had a place to stay. When I shook my head, he went into action. He consulted with customers and passersby about a suitable pension for me. The discussions were long and heated, punctuated with frequent exclamations of *"Merde!"*, that wonderfully apt word for all human seasons, and all excesses and insufficiencies.

Finally, they reached a consensus. Maurice led me to a house nearby. The pension was simple and clean, and the woman who showed us the room was warm and friendly. Maurice repeated my story to her and she at once declared her sympathy in the cause of *l'amour*. Maurice insisted I go to bed and practically tucked me in. I fell into a deep sleep.

I woke up a few hours later, took a bath, changed into fresh clothes, and felt the better for it.

I went to Maurice's café and everyone cheered at my appearance.

"Vive l'amour! Vive l'amour!"

Bolstered by this enthusiastic response, I headed for the small grey house. I knocked on the door, and waited.

Almost at once, the old woman opened the door. She had a huge smile on her face. I followed her through a small courtyard to a modest salon. A middle-aged couple introduced themselves as Le Comte and Comtesse Fournier. They were both simply dressed, soft-spoken and polite. Fortunately, they also spoke passable English. Hadley came in with the old woman. She gave a whoop of surprise and we hugged each other briefly and decorously.

We then all sat down for a talk under Le Comte's amiable direction. He said everyone present was aware of the situation and it was his hope that an amicable understanding be mutually arrived at. There should be no animosity. He had spoken to His Excellency, the Ambassador, who had granted him the authority to act as he saw fit. Le Comte was fair and diplomatic. He did not stir the coals but presented terms that I accepted at once. He assumed that I would at all times vouchsafe Mademoiselle's well-being and good reputation. I agreed to this and he thanked me, adding that I had his trust. I could see Hadley at reasonable times, but she must not stay out later than 10 o'clock. These formalities over, we were given permission to go out that afternoon.

Once outside and the door closed behind us, Hadley and I gave expression to our elation. We yelped with joy. I took her to meet Maurice and he and his friends embraced us and congratulated us. It was like a holiday. Hadley and I held hands at the small table and sipped our cappuccinos. Afterwards she took me on a tour of the town. It truly was charming. What appealed to me was the sense of human intimacy, the more humane scale of the old buildings. Here, man was not dwarfed by man-made structures, no false intimidating grandeur. By the late afternoon, we were both tired and I delivered her home at the decent hour of six.

I returned to the pension and took a brief nap before venturing out to dine. There were still some vestigial colours in the sky, lingering as if to put off the finality of day. A softness enveloped the town, made it mellow. Smiles came easily to faces and settled there awhile. The air scented with herbs and pine coaxed me to sweet slumber that night.

I woke up early the next day and went to the café. There, I whiled away an hour with Maurice, exchanging English for French. The croissant and *chocolat chaud* was a dream, a suitable bonus for getting up, coming into consciousness of the world. That particular morning, the weather was fair, the temperature cool, the sky a cloudless azure, a vast expanse over the whole terrain, over the scented mountains. I went to Le Comte's to fetch Hadley, and together, we headed for the hills. We stopped to buy some provisions on the way.

We came upon a prospect of Montagne Sainte-Victoire, instantly recognizable as the subject of so many paintings by Cézanne. In real life, Montagne Sainte-Victorie was not at all awesome. It was a friendly mass of stone, made violet by the special light, or magic in the air. It looked rather like a child's mountain, a piece of fairy-land. There it was, ahead, in the midst of the sweeping panorama of the Provençal countryside. We proceeded to climb eastwards to the rocky hillsides above the Château Noir. We clambered up a big boulder till we found a screen of trees. Another setting for Cézanne's brush. Besides the views, it was made special and memorable by the pleasant scent from the indigenous herbs sprouting about the countryside: oregano and thyme, mint and sage. A veritable feast for the senses.

I unpacked the small knapsack and spread our lunch on the ground. Sunlight poured onto us, directly from above. We had bought *fromage* — a hard local cheese, a soft cheese, red apples, a red Provençal dip, a large baguette, a bottle of local red wine, rated three stars, and a small thermos of fragrant coffee, courtesy of Maurice. "For *l'amour*," he had teased.

The food was delicious and sustaining: the apples crisp and slightly tart, as apples ought to be, and the wine full-bodied. We lay down side by side, on our backs, the foliage screening us from the direct rays of the winter sun, a playful breeze toying with the leaves.

We held hands. What more could one ask for? I felt so full. A sudden, rising surge of love and tenderness overwhelmed me which insisted on demonstration: I must kiss her! So I leant over her, my lips coming close to hers. She turned away from me, a definite gesture.

Tension mounted immediately between us, and we returned to our original positions, lying on our backs, parallel to each other. There was an angry, dirty silence, pregnant with danger. The ground at once uncomfortable with small pebbles and tree twigs which had been snatched off the branches by someone or something with a deliberate intention. But we did not shift away, as if nailed to the hard ground.

When the subsidence of my heart's palpitation allowed speech, I asked, "Now what was that about?"

"I don't know. You tell me what that was all about?" she swung back, a resistance in her voice.

"You avoided my kiss. You rejected me!"

"I'm not rejecting you. Don't be so silly."

"Don't you call me silly. You can't deny it. You avoided me as if I was s-s-some undesirable lout." My heated temper was causing me to stutter, which made everything worse.

"I'm sorry. I guess I wasn't ready for that."

"How could you brush me off as if I was an insect!"

"Please don't exaggerate. As I said, you must give me time. I'm not yet ready for a physical bond."

"And when is that going to be?"

"Please don't pressure me. When I'm not ready, I'm just not ready."

"This is just hunky dory!" This was a favourite expression of Hadley's.

"Don't be so petulant. It does not become you."

"This is just hunky dory," I repeated. I felt my argument weakening. I was fast turning into a petulant insect.

"Don't be so angry with me. I was brought up strictly by my mother," she said.

"The dragon lady enters the stage!"

"I can't talk to you when you're like this. Treat my mother with some decency, some respect! Although I don't always agree with her, I trust she acts for my interests."

"And how about her treatment of me? She's turning you into a virgin bride!"

Hadley did not respond to this. She would not speak to me again. Never! I too, could play this game. I shall out-silence her. So, in that brilliant afternoon of scented light on one of the most beautiful mountains in the world, two foolish lovers were struck dumb and mute from pride. Instead of making up, we remained silent, stubborn, shoring up our defence mechanisms. By the time we left, within the hour, our faces had darkened, and we were ready to despise. On the way to Le Comte's, Hadley said she would find her own way back, and before I could respond, had turned down another street. I was dumbfounded. I did not go after her.

Back in my room, I felt the wind pass through me: my skull hollow, my ribcage hollow. It lulled me to sleep. A merciful act. Another one of nature's comforts.

What am I doing in this strange room, on this stranger's bed? What have I done? Why am I sulking like a spoilt brat, just because my love would not kiss me? Just a kiss, was all I asked. What kind of love is this, a love without touching? She had no right to treat me as though I was a sex fiend. I wasn't even thinking of sex. Honest. Anyway, after awhile, I decided to phone and appease. Easy enough. The act of contrition always works. And so that evening, we met outside the café, and to appear reconciled, kissed and made up for all to witness. Clap clap. They clapped their hands! And the love story supposedly continues. And all's right with the world.

We spent the next day walking, walking. Seeing sights, visiting the tapestry museum, acting like happy tourists. Cynical snob! Yes, nothing wrong with being happy tourists.

Something had changed, the whole thing had changed. The immediacy was stunning. One moment this, the next, not like this. How to describe it? Well, it was like leaving a cup of hot coffee on the table. When you return, it had gotten cold. It had become a different cup of coffee, the coffee grounds blemishing the bottom of the white coffee cup with black, charred stars. Anyway, she would be departing soon, accompanying Le Comte and Comtesse on a vacation to the Riviera.

There were still good times: the night we went to the travelling carnival, the big tent erected just before the thick of continental darkness descended. We rode the mad roller-coaster, spun up on the gaily-lit Ferris wheel, ate candy floss which stuck to our faces. But it was all too contrived, like our relationship.

I departed two days later.

In Dublin I tried to return to my routine, but found it difficult. It was as if I had been given a wrong and bizarre script. I could make neither head nor tail of it. I was suffering from disorientation and fatigue. I would sit all day, desultorily, in noisy places, but could not decipher the babble of voices drowning the air. I was withdrawing from the world.

"Why so glum and gloomy?" It was Claude de Vere Browne, who'd just entered the Coffee Inn.

"Bugger off, Claude! Leave me alone. I don't want any company."

"What a way to greet a friend! Such a temper, despite your loved one's return! Aha! I guess you don't know about this!"

At once, I was on my Lambretta, heading for Dalkey. I had nothing worked out in my mind. I nearly ran into the dragon lady at the front entrance. She looked at me with an ambiguous smile.

"I presume you've come for Hadley?"

I just stood there, not knowing what to do.

"I'll go get her," she said confidently. It was almost as if she had won a victory.

When Hadley emerged, I looked at her and knew that I had lost, and that whatever followed was superfluous. Yet we acted out the conventions.

"You know it'll never work, don't you? It's a matter of time before we find that out. We're too different, you and I, and our worlds are different."

"Let's stop debating the issue. No point flogging a dead horse. Tell me honestly, is there someone else?"

She hesitated, then replied, "Yes, there's someone."

"Is he a cowboy?"

"His name is Bill."

"Is he a cowboy?"

She shook her head and laughed. "No, Bill's in law school at UCLA."

"A pity. I was hoping that he is a cowboy. That'll be just desserts for the dragon lady! I can visualize the scene. Your old lady watching as our hero, old Bill, the rugged cowboy, carries you away into the sunset on his faithful palomino, Spotted Iron."

"Oh please don't carry on about my mother."

"Where did you meet the lawyer?"

"Stop it! I'm leaving. This instant!"

"Wait! Before you vanish into your new bliss, there's the matter concerning my letters."

"What on earth are you talking about now?"

"The letters that I wrote you. I want them back!"

"That's a nutty request. Surely the letters are mine! You wrote them for me. They're mine now!"

"No, they're mine! Give them back!"

"You're a joker, expecting me to give them back. Besides, I can't give them back even if I want to…"

"What do you mean?" I had a sinking feeling before she spoke.

"Well, I burnt them."

"Aaaahhhh, you wanton witch! How could you do that to me? Leaving me is alright. That, I can bear. But to burn my letters!!! That, I can never forgive you. Never!"

"Why are you making such a big deal over a pile of old letters?"

"Because they contain my very life! Those letters, which you treat so slightingly, contain original poems, or their early drafts. In many instances, they are the only copies I ever made."

"That was a stupid thing to do. I'm sorry this happened. Didn't you memorize them?"

Now that just wasn't worthy of a reply.

"Tell me, why did you burn them?"

"Because it wouldn't be fair to Bill. Besides, I couldn't stand many of them. Probably, on hindsight, they were the true reason for our break-up. You were so negative, so angry, so bleak."

"My, so many adjectives."

"So unpredictable, so impulsive, so mad. For instance, if I were to ask you to jump into the icy water of the sea right now, you would do so, without thinking, without hesitation!"

"Well, ask me!"

"Alright, go jump in the sea!"

"OK. I'll jump in the sea!"

I immediately disrobed myself of every article of clothing and handed them to her. She laughed and screamed and tried to dissuade me.

I strode down to the beach, the air cold against my body, the first crop of goose-pimples erupting on my skin. I considered enough was enough. Time to stop playing the fool.

"Stop! Come on back!" she cried. "You're mad, mad!"

Under these circumstances, I had to go on, although each step into deeper water was uncomfortable, if not painful. My progress was slow. When I reached waist height, I felt my balls freeze and remember thinking, I could be the first man to be castrated by the cold sea that dying year.

117

I moved deeper and seized by a recklessness, plunged headlong into the water. It was terribly cold but, at the same time, exhilarating. Hadley was still yelling on shore that dark evening, but I felt heroic. I tried to look like a hero, and not a wimp who had just lost his girl to a cowboy called Bill. I shivered visibly, detracting from the visage I wanted to present to my ex-beloved one.

Back on land and dressed, there was nothing more to say. We walked away from each other. When we were some distance apart, I thought I heard her call out, "I loved you." I must have been mistaken.

Seaward, I saw something move on the water. I approached.

It was at swim, one bird.

One Summer at
Cloch na Rón

I HAD NOT YET TURNED seventeen when my parents sent me abroad to study in Dublin.

But why Ireland? Perhaps it was because Dublin had a reputable university and medical school and was thought to be cheaper to live in than England or the USA. But what truly swayed my parents, however, was their presumption that holy Catholic Ireland was a safer place for their impressionable young son, less likely to lead him astray. Although they were not Christians, they believed every religion was good and ethical and who would cavil about that?

However, they were wrong. Dublin was not that cheap after all, and it certainly was not safe for the morals of a young foreign student. Within a year, I had converted to Roman Catholicism, downed my first pint of Guinness, puffed my first cigarette, kissed my first girl, and written my first poem.

I succumbed to Catholicism on account of acute loneliness and homesickness when I was enrolled that very first year at Blackrock College, a boarding school run by the Holy Ghost fathers. It was more sensibility than sense, and my romantic nature, that made me respond to the religious rites and rituals of the church. I loved the dim, hallowed spaces, the light made soft filtering through panes of colourful stained glass, the odour of incense and the choral music. The atmosphere of these rituals moved me more than true spiritual conviction or doctrinal certainty. Often, the beauty of the church services brought tears to my eyes. I felt as if I was on the threshold of a nameless and indescribable holiness. I was eager to do good works, joined the Legion of Mary and even contemplated becoming a monk. However, I was soon swamped by my studies at the medical school at University College, Dublin.

Leaving boarding school after a long year was like suddenly being freed. Not surprisingly, I could not deal sensibly with this new freedom. An empty vessel eager to be filled, I went after life with great avidity like a piranha for every indiscriminate morsel of flesh, even gobbling up the bones.

In no time at all, I was in my element in the pubs of Dublin, drinking Guinness as well as the next man. I smoked a pipe, or fiddled with it, and read books till my brow furrowed. I became a sceptic and developed a disposition to doubt everything, including my newfound Catholicism. I fell from grace as rapidly as I had gained it. In succession, I rebelled against colonialism, neo-colonialism, capitalism, communism, the Irish Press and Hollywood movies. I adopted a distaste for all authority or orthodoxy, and changed my opinions, beliefs, values, more often than I changed my clothes.

I was living out the tumultuous clashes between the cultures of the East and the West. At that age, they were an unequal match. I was overwhelmed by the Western World, swamped by its newspapers, radio, theatre, cinema and books, books, books. So that after awhile, I staggered about in a shell-shocked dance down the road towards deculturalization and cultural pariahdom, as though it were all fun and games. My mind was blown away when I saw myself in lines like Samuel Beckett's "The sun shone, having no alternative, on the nothing new. Murphy sat out of it, as though he were free."

Ever susceptible, ever gullible, I fell for the intellectual and philosophical fashions in vogue at that time in the West: namely, existentialism and the notion of the absurd — unavoidable, if one frequented the pubs and the coffee houses.

I became a person whose feet were no longer planted on the ground, to my peril. I inhabited the world of books while shunning the real world, something that did not stand me in good stead in later life.

Although I regarded myself as shy, nevertheless I made friends. Those days in Dublin, it was easy enough to meet people. All one had to do was to patronize certain pubs and coffee houses in the vicinity of Grafton Street. The legendary talkers loved to practise the art of repartee. They held court and drew loyal crowds about them.

Joan and Garry Trimble counted among my best friends. They were both architects in their mid-thirties, with two young daughters and a grey-striped kitten. They were part of the crowd I mixed with: poets and novelists, journalists, students, artists, musicians, members of the Teilifís Eireann, Ireland's national broadcasting company, and the theatre. Garry was also a well-known sculptor specializing in bronze busts. As a sign of his distinction, he had been commissioned to execute a bust of Éamon de Valera, the Taoiseach or head of government, who later became President of Ireland, a tall thin domineering man whose powers towered above everyone else's.

Garry was kind and gregarious, with big baby-blue eyes that stared at the world, agog with wonder and disbelief. He sported a hair-lick always flopping teasingly down over his forehead which he constantly brushed aside with his hand, like Bill Haley, the famous Rock and Roll singer with the Rockets, popular in the 50s.

Sweet and obliging, Garry was always willing to do favours for others, transporting them in his small, yellow Volkswagen to and from parties or the airport. Dublin those days was a party-town. Nightly, there was bound to be at least one party one could attend. No one was turned away provided they brought their "passport" — half a dozen bottles of porter or a bottle of cheap Spanish wine. In every pub, the buzz was "Where's the party? Where's the party?" reaching a crescendo as the night wore on. At pub-closing time, crowds of excited and drunken revellers would pile into cars and roar out to the party. That was a dangerous hour to be walking in the street as the party-goers, night-fevered and soused, made their way out of Grafton Street and its environs. Once they were gone, an eerie silence descended on the town.

One time when I took ill, Garry came to check on me daily, made me hot soups and coffee, brought newspapers and magazines, related the latest gossip and scandals. My nurse and newshound but affectionate as a puppy.

Joan was a bright, warm, empathetic soul whom I trusted and to whom I confided my deepest secrets. We developed a special bond, Joan becoming my first close and platonic woman friend.

I spent a lot of time at the Trimbles' house, a small, converted, mews cottage in Ballsbridge, a desirable quarter of the town. I often dined with them, sometimes cooking curry or Chinese food which they appreciated. Afterwards, we would loll on the hardwood floor, comfortably buttressed by big throw cushions and pillows. We loved drinking wine, talking till the proverbial cows waltzed home. Sometimes, I would sleep over, or babysit their daughters when they had an engagement.

They had built a small cottage near a village in Connemara which they loved. They spoke of the villagers with affection. The natives in that part of Connemara spoke Gaelic and a dialect of English few outsiders could understand. They had ingeniously and wonderfully corrupted the Queen's English, taking great liberties with it so that it became craggy like the mountains, rough like the coast, lyrical like the wind. This interested and excited me, for by then, I had decided to write in the English foisted upon me by the quirks of history.

I think it was Yeats who described Connemara as a land of incorrigible beauty. A desolate landscape with old, bare hills, stones and craggy shores, right on the Atlantic. I wanted to go there. I was ready to be enchanted.

The opportunity came in the long summer vacation of 1956. Summer vacation was one of the boons of being a student. Although I did not have the wherewithal to do much, the largesse of weeks of unstructured time, of escaping the schedule of the medical student, with lectures and tutorials in the classrooms, demonstrations and clinical rounds at the teaching hospital and long hours in the library, was nothing short of heaven sent. It also meant that I had time to pursue other interests, especially reading.

I jumped at the chance when Joan and Garry offered their cottage, saying I could stay as long as I wished that summer. My bones sang for the green hills, the blue sea, the vast open sky.

❧

I set off one fine summer day, ready to meet bards and druids in the wilds of Connemara. The coach drove through the patchwork of green and yellow fields, lush pastures, just the scenery associated with the Emerald Isle. Throughout the journey, the sky was overcast. In Galway, I changed to another coach bound for Clifden. The weather turned more sombre by the minute, the waters of Lake Corrib were a black sheet, the road twirled around the foot of high, dark mountains, their bald peaks barely visible in the fading light. When the coach came to the coastal stretch, I could see and hear the wild surf of the Atlantic pounding jagged rocks, black as misery. When we finally reached Cloch na Rón, a heavy shower enveloped the small village.

I disembarked onto the rag ends of the day. There was not a soul in sight on the streets and the whole village wore an inhospitable and desolate air. I headed towards the church which stood on the rise dominating the village. Its sharp steeple pierced above the houses, the tip not quite reaching heaven. There was nothing striking or beautiful about the structure, and that went for the village itself. Cloch na Rón lacked charm. For a moment, I wondered if I had come to the wrong place. I felt very far from home, far from the glitter and friendliness of Dublin. I looked about me. The area inspired the thought that God had put us on this world solely to suffer. A cold, stony vale of tears.

Salt rain stung my eyes. I inhaled a deep breath of the briny air and went on. I approached a house squatting alongside the church, which I surmised to be the residence of the parish priest. I walked up the flagstone path, pressed the doorbell and waited. I heard the sound of light footsteps. The door opened. Yellow light from within flowed out through the open door to strike at this stranger. A small, old woman with mousy-brown hair studied me. Fine lines criss-crossed her face.

"Good evening! I am looking for Father Fergus Cassidy."

"Well, c'mon in! Come in this moment out of the rain. Hand me your coat. It's dripping wet."

She took my coat and hung it in the closet.

"I'm afraid Father Cassidy's stepped out for the evening."

"I've brought a note of introduction from the Trimbles," I said and gave her my name.

"I'm Miss Dunne, the housekeeper. We've been expecting you. I've made a bed for you in the front room. I'm going to warm up your supper. It'll not take long. Let me show you to your room."

She had the brisk walk of small women, her limbs moving quickly. She carried about her an air of severity, her long-sleeved white cotton blouse had a high collar which seemed to be strangling her, her gruff voice fighting the constriction. A long black skirt trailed down to her ankles. She showed me into a spacious room with a bay window which looked out on the street below. The heavy, green curtains were drawn back.

"Supper will be on the table in half an hour. I'll be calling you."

"Shouldn't I wait for Father Cassidy?"

"You won't want to do that. The Father has stepped out to a party. Lord knows when he'll be back. He took his instrument."

"Instrument?" I asked, puzzled.

"Aye, his instrument. The accordion."

"Ah, yes! Mr. and Mrs. Trimble did tell me that the Father's fond of music, and that he's a good tenor."

"Aye, that he does. Singing. And dancing too. He likes to see people dance."

"Sounds like a jolly chap."

"Perhaps, perhaps. He's a bit too easygoing, to my mind."

"His parishioners are pretty lucky to have such a jovial and fun-loving spiritual guardian."

"But it's not good, is it? No one's afraid of him."

"But why should people be afraid of him?"

"Because he's the Lord's priest, that's why! He's Jesus Christ's representative on this patch of earth!" With that, she turned abruptly and swept out of my presence with that brisk scissoring of her legs.

I strolled over to the wide window. Still not a soul in sight. The wind blew the rain aslant. Yellow halos glowed around every street lamp. The village remained uninviting. I turned to face the room, dominated by a huge bed squatting regally on wooden legs with castors. More suitable for a gross couple, or a whole family, than the thin bones and insubstantial flesh of a young Asian student. There was something forbidding about the room, the bare white walls adding to the feeling of austerity, its sole adornment a wooden crucifix hung above the bed-board. It bore the wearied, pain-torn body of Christ, his sorrowful head tilted, looking down directly at the occupant of the bed. That could deter passion and lust, having God as witness to the act!

Then I noticed an unlabelled bottle on the bedside table. Propped against it was a note to me, penned with a flourishing hand. Big and legible.

A bottle of the good stuff for your enjoyment, the best in all creation, say the local connoisseurs. Alas, I know my flock too well, that they are prone to exaggeration. It's a habit elevated into a cultural attribute. I fight on alone. God be on my side!

Looking forward to a nice and agreeable piece of chat tomorrow morning after mass.

Yours in Christ, Fergus Cassidy.

Bless the man, he had presented me with a bottle of poteen, the real, old stuff. Sinful and unlawful as hell, but many, including myself, would go some ways to risk hell for the good brew. And from a parish priest in Connemara, it would be matchless! Something really good to look forward to, a tot after dinner. And then it dawned on me that there was no good reason why I should not have a tot before dinner. On earth, we all need a tot now and then, to boost one's spirit with the spirit. Yes, yes, I would risk hell for it again.

I poured out a good measure and raised it to my nostrils to get a better whiff of it. I held it against the ceiling light and it was clear, translucent, with just that hint of rust. I took in a mouthful, swirled it around with a keen sense of appreciation, even of reverence, in tribute to its power and beauty. When I swallowed it, the whole bolus descended like live lava down my gullet towards the stomach. Straight away, it settled me and I felt stronger, more relaxed.

The sorcery of alcohol! The natural need for mankind to be intoxicated. Now and then at least, or to consecrate a wedding or a birth, that is why every nation learns to brew arak, mescal, maotai, whisky, samsu, vodka and kirsch, as many brews as there are tribes of man.

There was a knock on the door.

"Supper's on the table!"

"Thanks Miss Dunne. I'm coming."

The dining room was filled with massive pieces of wooden furniture. The long, oblong table was made to seat 12, almost baronial. On it were cold cuts of mutton, boiled cabbage, spuds made golden with country butter, their delicious hot steam rising from the dish. There was a jug of thick, rich brown gravy.

I helped myself to a generous plateful of meat and potatoes and then pitched a fork-full into my mouth. "Very good," I pronounced appreciatively.

"There's hot drinking water and tea on the table and brown bread I baked on first rising this morning."

While I ate, Miss Dunne busied herself wiping and polishing the furniture until it shone. A piece of soft cloth in hand, she moved constantly from one article to another, wiping and polishing. I could imagine Miss Dunne wandering around the house all day, giving everything in her path the same treatment. I could see a long life of service in Miss Dunne, I could.

"Does it rain here often, Miss Dunne?"

"Aye, that it does, surely."

"Hope it will clear tomorrow and be a fine day. I'm going to the Trimbles' cottage."

"God willin'."

"Does Cloch na Rón attract a lot of visitors in the summer?"

"Visitors? Well, I don't know. Don't meet many meself. I dunno. What's there to see here? Only a hard life, is all."

"There must be something special about Cloch na Rón and Connemara that draws people here."

"Special!" She almost spat out the words. "Why, we've only a hard life here, and with God's help, get through it without going mad. But most times, it's black and bitter. Aye, life is surely a vale of tears."

I was too young then to disagree. I felt that I had barely begun to live and the future was bright with promise. No, I did not think that life was entirely a vale of tears. I felt so vividly alive and I ate hungrily. The housekeeper paid me no more heed but remained in the room, wiping and polishing away.

When I finished, Miss Dunne cleared the table and before leaving the room, announced that Father Cassidy would be celebrating mass at 7.30 sharp the next morning. Breakfast would be served after mass.

"Thank you, I shall be up."

"If you are turning in, I bid ye goodnight and God bless." She made the sign of the cross, blessing me.

"Goodnight Miss Dunne, and thanks again." I watched her as she returned quietly to the kitchen. I fancied her life was pretty circumscribed by this house, that there was not much outside it to entice this reticent woman. I suspected that she was used to boundaries, in this country of stone walls ringing in pastures and fields.

Back in the bedroom, I changed and climbed into the huge bed. I took up J.M. Synge's *Riders to the Sea*. That black night, the wind driving the rain against the window panes accentuated the atmospherics described in the book. Set in the Aran Islands nearby, the landscape and its people were not dissimilar to Cloch na Rón's. How strange to find myself in this faraway part of the world with its wild turbulent seas, and the hardy people who challenged it daily.

I woke up early the next morning, went across to the wide window and peeked at the world outside. A dull grey morning, not quite the sort of trumpeting day to advance upon a journey.

ℤ❧

Entering the* high portals of the church, I blessed myself with holy water from the stone stoup, made the sign of the cross and silently recited: "*Asperges me, Domine, hyssop et mundabor, Lavabis me, et super nivem dealbabor.*" "Thou shalt sprinkle me with hyssop, O Lord, and I shall be cleansed, Thou shalt wash me and I shall be whiter than snow."

I walked slowly down the centre aisle, made the sign of the cross again, genuflected and slid quietly into the long wooden bench. Although not a Sunday or a special feast day, there was a full congregation. The church was alive and well in Connemara in 1956.

A general hush soon descended on the congregation. Some were mouthing personal prayers, others sat or knelt in contemplative silence, with an air of reverence and piety. Father Cassidy entered and proceeded to the altar followed by his server. He was wearing white vestments trimmed in green and gold, a chasuble over his stole and a black biretta on his head. The server was a young boy about ten years old, with cherubic pink cheeks, dressed in a white surplice.

The mass began with the priest sprinkling holy water at the congregation, making the sign of the cross as he intoned: "*In nomine Patris et Filli et Spiritus Sancti. Amen. Introibo ad altare Dei.*"

As I followed the celebration of the mass, I was surprised that my participation was not entirely mechanical and that I felt a certain reverence. In those days, the Catholic mass was celebrated in Latin universally, which enhanced the mysterious, magical quality of the ritual. In matters of religion, in our congress with God, perspicuity is not needed. Perfect comprehension is not necessary. What is needed is a leap of faith, to embrace the unknown, the unknowable. Blessed are the faithful.

That morning, the mass flowed along like a blessed river. Despite the vanity and pride which had brought about my denial of God, I found myself awed, reverent, and moved to prayer. I just could not stop talking to God, wanting to believe it all, reconcile this life with the life hereafter, solve that big puzzle about life and death once and for all.

Practically the whole congregation rose and lined up for Holy Communion with a look of expectancy and of bliss. How I envied them. They seemed transformed after receiving the Body of Christ, their countenances registering peace and an inner innocence, even the glow of ecstasy. I felt unblessed, lonely and bereft.

Back at the parish house, I sat down to breakfast with Father Cassidy. The Father was fresh and relaxed after the mass as if he had just emerged from a bath. He was a handsome man in his early fifties, boyish, full of zeal, with a shock of white hair and the solid build of a former rugby player. I thanked him for his hospitality and for the bottle of poteen.

"Did you like it?" he asked eagerly. "It came from a highly regarded source. This parishioner of mine can brew bootleg like an angel."

"Like the devil more likely!" commented Miss Dunne, who was hovering nearby.

There was black tea, strong, the way the Irish love it. There was brown bread fresh from the oven, country butter and strawberry jam. There were fried eggs, rashers of bacon and rich black pudding on my plate.

"Miss Dunne's a harsh judge of people," laughed Father Cassidy.

"And ye yourself's a soft judge, you are," Miss Dunne countered.

"She'll likely consign everybody to the pits of Hell," Father Cassidy continued.

"Aye, and they'll only be getting their just desserts!"

"And how are our mutual friends, the Trimbles?"

"They're just fine. They send you their regards."

"A lovely couple, a lovely couple, God bless them."

"Yes, indeed."

"I spoke to Garry just the other day and we talked about your coming. He mentioned that you're a medical student and that you write poetry."

I always felt an excitement tinged with embarrassment when anyone talked about my writing. I had not written much, as yet, and nothing well enough to be labelled a writer. All I had was a wish, a passion to write truthfully, whatever that meant. Or perhaps it was only a conceit?

"I've written nothing worthwhile ..."

Ignoring this, Father Cassidy continued, "What language do you write in?"

"English!" I said. "But my mother tongue is Chinese, or more accurately, Fukienese. I was enrolled in an English-language school soon after the war, after the Japanese surrendered and Malaya became again part of the British Empire, on which the sun never sets. So we were taught English. My parents' generation understood that if one wanted to get on in life, a grasp of the English language was essential."

"So the British did to your people what they did to mine. You see, before Independence which we'd fought for and won in 1922, they dominated Ireland for 700 years! At one time our people were forbidden to buy land, speak Irish or Gaelic, or practise their religion freely. We practically lost our own language. It now exists with a conscious struggle, only in pockets of our blessed country called the Gaeltacht, of which Connemara is a proud part."

"Yes," I said. "The British, like all colonizers, treated their subjects shabbily. We also have a long list of grievances."

"And you want to write in English?" the priest chided with a hint of mischief.

"It can't be helped. It's too late now. The damage is done. Now I speak and read English better than I do Chinese. Like Pandit Nehru, I lament that I even dream in English. And I was taught more than just the English language: I studied their literature and history as well as their politics and their God. I've been transformed into a Wog."

"A Wog? What's that?"

"A W O G — a Westernized Oriental Gentleman!"

We shared a friendly laugh. "The same goes for us Irish. Despite the rise of nationalism and the instalment of the Irish Free State, the expression of the Irish people is being promulgated through its writers in the English language, an alien, master tongue! You're probably familiar with the so-called Irish literary renaissance led by Yeats, Lady Gregory, George Moore and others ..."

I noted that Father Cassidy had omitted Joyce, O'Casey and Beckett, my own favourite writers of the day. Although seldom mentioned, these three had, voluntarily or involuntarily, lived outside Ireland. They chose self-exile.

We finished breakfast and Miss Dunne cleared the table.

"Tell me, my son, why do you want to be a writer?" he flashed me a genial smile.

"Don't really know, Father. Don't think I can give you a straightforward simple answer. The source of writing's a mystery to me. It's magic."

"Surely the source is divine, is God himself?" stated the priest.

"Perhaps it is, perhaps the source is God. Taking everything into consideration, it's almost impossible to rule this out."

"I don't catch you, rule what out?" Father Cassidy asked. From his tone and demeanour, I suspected that the priest was getting ready to challenge me.

"Why, to rule out the existence of a central intelligence, or of God if you will," I baited him. "I've tried to find out how the great masters define poetry. Some claim it was an antidote to man's loneliness and his mortality. Others claimed that poetry was an exertion in demonstration of man's free will. I have little experience, being still young, but I think they might all be right. However, I usually find academia and cleverness rather odious. Anything connected to poetry is difficult but is worthwhile because its aim is ingenious delight."

"Do you think that poetry gives all the answers?"

"No, not quite, but then are answers all that important?"

"How can you say that! Surely they are all important!" Father Cassidy plunked his empty teacup down. He leaned forward, planting his elbows on the table as if ready to engage in arm-wrestling.

"Sometimes, I wonder whether questions are that important."

The priest, thus happily provoked, eyes sparkling in anticipation, stated, "If you truly believe that questions are unimportant and answers as well, why, then you may be no better than a piece of rock, or a sheep in the field!"

"Yes," I deliberated. "I can accept that we are no better than a rock or a sheep."

"But man has been created by God, and He has sent His Son to us in man's image, to save our souls. Surely, we believe that God created us to be higher beings than a rock or a sheep. God created order and our main essential quest is to find order and to find God. We all aspire to be in God's presence, in His domain, and the nearer we are to Him, the greater the order."

"On the contrary, I think that perhaps Hell is the most orderly place. I am considering prisons, authoritative or dictatorial societies where men control other men, when men are made slaves."

I noticed that Miss Dunne was still in the room, wiping the wooden sideboard with a white rag. She had been listening to our debate but I could not hazard what she thought of it all.

"Are you then an anarchist?"

"I don't think so."

"Well, you are still young, and it's natural for the young to rebel. I hope I don't sound too patronizing, but reading indiscriminately can be dangerous, especially reading the wrong books. And the kind of company you keep, of course. Let's face it, one can be led astray, especially by the devil." The priest was being patronizing and I did not reply. "Too many writers these days are sceptical and display hostility towards the church. You should read Cardinal Newman. He's a good writer, and he has a fine mind. I'll get you my copy of the *University*. You'll find a lot of nourishment there."

I shrugged, noncommittal.

"I can't claim to have read a great deal of literature, therefore my knowledge isn't large. In my humble office as priest to my flock of sinners, I am swamped by everyday problems, with mundane issues, with reality. While literature belongs more to the realm of the imagination, of invention. Something contrived, no?"

It was pointless to argue, so I refrained from the debate. I had become a snob!

Father Cassidy said pleasantly, "I enjoy Dickens and Belloc." However, he divulged that his favourite book was *St. Augustine's Confessions*.

This drew a smile from me. I recalled reading *St. Augustine* and was amused by his notorious prayer, "O Lord, give me chastity and continence, but not yet!"

"My old Rector at the Jesuit seminary I attended was a personal friend of Father John Hopkins, but I found his poetry hard to read. Sprung rhythm!"

I did not respond, and at this point, Miss Dunne slid silently from the dining room like a shadow. I felt she disapproved of my behaviour and that made me unhappy.

"How long will you be in Connemara?"

"To be honest, I don't know. I have no rigid plans. Could stay a week or a month," I answered.

"Hope there's a chance for us to meet again. I don't often have the opportunity to talk to someone intelligent from the outside world. We lead a narrow life here, a small life. The land and the sea round hereabouts are what we know best. Our lives depend on it. We are painfully poor, as you will find. Perhaps we are not yet fully recovered from the Great Famine, which brought so much suffering. All in all, during that disaster of 1847, a million Irish died, and a million and a half chose emigration to America. There's still a sadness, a constant melancholy, which sits on us."

"Yes," I said softly, "I've read about the Great Famine."

"I must tell you that the people of Cloch na Rón have little knowledge of the outside world except for America where some of our people have migrated. Don't take offence if they stare. It will be out of curiosity, not malice. You will find them not unfriendly."

"Thank you, Father. I'll try and remember. I'm looking forward to making friends and finding out more about the people here."

"The majority are small farm holders, often of less than five acres. Through hard labour, they can only scratch a living from the stony soil. Others brave the hazards of the sea. I'm praying that we can develop tourism. There's a great deal of arts and crafts and culture in these parts, and the landscape is magnificent. One of my dreams is to organize an Arts Festival and invite Princess Grace of Monaco to come and open the first one."

Suddenly, I liked this man of God, this man of man. I said to him, "I heard that you are a fine tenor, Father."

"Ah, that's all my mother's doing, God be with her. She was the great singer in our family. When she was alive, there was singing coming out of the chimney all the day long. It was from that wonderful and happy woman, that we got our love for music. Me Da' was as musically deaf as the stones in the fields. Nowadays, some of us gather at kitchen parties for a bit of singing and dancing. All very harmless. Perhaps you'd like to come. You can sing us one of your national songs or offer a poem or two."

"I think, Father, I should be getting along. You are a busy man and I've already taken too much of your time. I'm grateful for your hospitality, not to mention your poteen."

"Well, it will help cheer you up on a cold night. Have you enough provisions and stuff?"

"Yes. All I need to buy are a few items in the village."

"You'll find there's precious little to buy here, after your city. And you need transportation to the Trimbles'. Three miles is hard on foot with all your baggage. Buses are few and far between, but I can arrange a lift for you with Nick Gallagher. I heard he's leaving for Clifden around noon. He'll give you a ride but you have to travel together with the carcasses. Nick's a butcher."

I readily accepted the offer. It was arranged that I would return to the rectory before noon.

I tramped down the stone-paved path to the jetty. The village was built smack on the side of a raised saddle of hills, the frontages of the houses facing the sea. The small whitewashed stone cottages with thatched roofs were all of identical design. The villagers looked sombre, and went about their daily chores with an air of submissiveness, of lives bowed down by poverty and piety. Yes, the heaviness, the great weight of God.

The jetty below the village was a great arm built of stone and concrete, embracing the mighty Atlantic, enfolding the vast water. That early morning, within its embrasure, half a dozen curraghs traced their paths upon the liquid skin of the water, the rowers making their exertions rhythmically. Outside, towards the horizon, the grey distance was dotted with islands. A soft wind came from the south, barely ruffling the ocean. Overhead, a good dozen white seagulls rode the invisible air with consummate grace. I walked out to the end of the jetty to take in the view.

⁓❧

Since childhood, the sea has always made me feel exultant.

The first time I saw the sea is indelibly etched in my memory. I was ten years old. It was about a year after the Second World War. My father, who was Technical Assistant at the Public Works Department, had rented a government holiday bungalow at Port Dickson for a week. The trip from Kuala Lumpur had taken two hours, passing through endless rubber plantations and small kampongs. Our old Riley automobile cramped with my parents and four children, climbed up the narrow winding stretch at Mantin Pass. Two of my sisters had travel sickness and the car had to stop at intervals to allow them to throw up by the side of the road. Finally, cresting a rise, we came upon the sea. My breath was taken away. That first sight of the expanse of blue under a wide bright sky filled me with ecstasy. My family must have felt a similar release of the spirit for we all broke spontaneously into song:

We were sailing along
On Moonlight Bay,
We can hear the voices ringing
They seemed to say ...

We sang loudly and joyously. Each subsequent time, whenever we journeyed to Port Dickson, we abandoned ourselves
in song whenever we topped the same rise and saw the sea.
For me, these were the best of all times in my family. I have
loved the sea ever since.

Now I looked out to a sea the colour of rain, a metallic
grey, so different from the turquoise of the tropics. Still, it
was the sea, and I stood on the jetty listening to the tongues
of water lapping the stony base, the lick and slurp. It was
low tide, the high water mark some three feet above the
present level. Rises and falls, the sea. Rises and recedes,
rhythmically.

Curraghs moved slowly across the body of water at their
intrinsic pace, the oars pushing at the surface, moving at the
pace of dream.

I stood watching a long while, my thoughts floating
upon time.

❧

At noon, Mr. Gallagher arrived in his lime-green Ford Anglia
van. I sat in front, my baggage at my feet, the rear was packed
with pig and sheep carcasses. A powerful smell of raw meat
and blood pervaded the interior of the van. Miss Dunne waved
us off.

Mr. Gallagher was a tall, thin, taciturn man, with big
sad eyes like a cow. We ran out of small talk before we had
left the village and endured an embarrassing silence between
us. Once past the outskirts of Cloch na Rón, we drove along
the coast road and followed the contours at the hem of the
mountains. We passed scattered stone cottages with thatched
roofs, small fields with straggles of sheep and the odd cow,

and here and there, a brace of the native Connemara ponies, the animals hemmed in by stone walls and fences, the stones picked by hand and stacked, the work of generations. I could make out the fretwork of sheep trails in the low corrugations of the potato plots. It was hard land to till and farm.

I remarked on the inhospitality of the land. Mr. Gallagher hugged his silence tight, then nodded and said, "Aye, nothin' much grows in these here parts. All we can grow here is heartaches."

Finally, we arrived at our destination. I got out, thanked the butcher, and the green van proceeded on its way. From where I stood on the road, the cottage could not be seen. Assorted rocks were strewn about the land like the effigies of abandoned deities. Some were like the works of Henry Moore. Grass grew sparsely among patches of furze and bracken. Not a tree was in sight.

The cottage was a square box constructed of stone, cement and glass, designed by Joan and Garry. It squatted across two big rocks, with a small stream coursing beneath. Inside, the white walls caught the light like an indoor pool that I could swim in. I immediately felt at home. There was a large living area with the kitchen at one end. A sofa faced the fireplace. A few simple wooden chairs stood around the dining table. A passage led to the two bedrooms and the bathroom. Spacious and bright. And I had the whole place to myself. What luxury!

Later, I went out to survey the terrain. The edge of the land plunged sharply downward to the sea. A loud primal roar rose to the sky as wave after wave unleashed by the ocean battered against the mammoth, black rocks before me. The violence was unrelenting, denoting the implacable will, the brutal might of God once again. At the nexus where sea and land and sky conjoined.

In the late afternoon, I sat in the small, sweet stream of bright water to wash myself. I lathered my body, then lay down in the stream to wash it off.

Back at the cottage, I lit a peat fire, a red, hot heart in the room. The flare projected reflections onto the walls, flickering dream flowers; nocturnal phantasmagoria conjured up by the fire.

I was hungry. I had not eaten since my breakfast with Father Cassidy. I took out a couple of lamb chops from the refrigerator, seasoned them and put them into the preheated oven. I scrubbed some potatoes and put them in water to boil. Fine-chopped onions were sprinkled onto the chops and then I cut cabbage for stir-fry.

I love cooking and I love eating. Back home, food was the strongest expression of the culture of my people. Although quite content with life as a student in Dublin, I missed good food. The better restaurants were beyond my means, so I was forced to cook.

From early childhood, the big kitchen cum dining room had been the true centre of my home. Mainly the domain of the women, I found it irresistible.

"Why do you want to be with us women? You will grow up to be a sissy! Go and play with the boys."

I thought this unjust, clear gender discrimination. I loved the kitchen. I watched with fascination as the women went about their chores: slitting the throats of chickens and ducks; flinging live carp against the hard cement floor to stun them; throwing wriggling crustaceans into boiling hot water to their silent deaths. They performed these skills without obvious squeamishness, even holding the chicken's neck as vivid red blood gushed out into the bowl.

In the midst of that torture and slaughter, the women chatted about their favourite classical Chinese opera stars. I would eavesdrop as they relished accounts of indiscretions, infidelities and scandals. Through my forays in the kitchen, I learnt not only to cook but also the endless complexities of the human species.

Then there was the noise, the continuous cacophony as they sliced and chopped, pounded and stirred, kneaded and patted, laughed and cursed. The language seemed shockingly crude, especially when it emerged from some shy, sloe-eyed cousin.

And the smells! The bewitching mix of garlic, chilli, pepper, cloves, cinnamon, cardamom, onions, lime, tamarind and fermented shrimp paste. All the odours of the Malayan kitchen.

My hunger grew enormous as I took the chops sizzling out of the oven. I sat and ate with gusto, then made a cup of coffee and went outside.

I felt the night contract about me. The sky was moonless and starless, so dark that I could make out nothing at first and groped about like a blind man, taking care with every step. I walked until I was in total darkness. The lit cottage in the distance, a ghost ship floating upon a black ocean. Under the spell of night, I was less than miniscule in relation to the vastness of the universe.

Sitting in that dark, I realized for the first time in my life that I was truly alone. Yet I did not feel lonely. On the contrary, I relished the solitude.

Then I imagined the firmament addressing me: "What are you saying? That you want eternal life?"

To the warm, maternal night, I answered that I was worth one life and that I accepted that.

Inside the cottage again, I added another brick of peat and poked about with the iron tongs. Sparks began to flare up here and there, soon coalescing into tongues of flames. I poured out half a tumbler of Father Cassidy's poteen and reclined on the sofa, watching the fire, stupefied. Gradually, my body sank into the cushions, everything soft, relaxed, doing nothing. Nothing. My eyes caressed the room without effort, till all memory faded from my mind. I had forgotten the world's perpetual dancing, its revolving. As the fire died down, down, the embers extinguished and brought the night in. I had one notion before I fell into sleep, and that was "I live here!"

The next morning, I got up with an urge to watch the sunrise. Wrapped in a blanket against the cold, I stumbled out into a dimly lit world. Behind the cottage, the mountain peaks were growing red in the dawn. Dew decorated the blades of grass. There was freshness and promise, the unveiling of Eden. Light swelled, streaming from the emerging sun into a world of abundance. Grey rocks stood like sentinels, the meadow sea green, small birds singing, air dancing over the sea. Soon, there was full sunlight and blue sky extended in every direction.

I washed in the cold water of the stream, then went indoors to change into a yellow T-shirt and a pair of shorts. I prepared a breakfast of oatmeal and milk, into which I sliced an apple. I made coffee and ate three slices of brown bread. Having eaten, I felt ready for the world.

This morning was different from other mornings, no longer yoked to time or plans. Not being governed by the means to an end, the means themselves becoming the end, I took off my wristwatch and put it away. That done, I felt liberated.

I went outdoors again and walked barefoot in the wet grass, drinking in the early moments of the day. I walked down to the bottom of the land, climbed up a large boulder by the water's edge where I had a clear view of the sea as it thundered against the shore. I was awed by the incredible power and force of nature. The pounding waves advanced and retreated endlessly, spray rose high in the air. I stayed there for some time, mesmerized. Then an inspiration! What an apt setting to read poetry out loud!

I hurried back and brought out a copy of Rilke's "Duino Elegies". I climbed up the big boulder again, took a deep breath and began to read the First Elegy:

Who, if I cried out, would hear me among the angels'
hierarchies? and even if one of them pressed me

suddenly against his heart: I would be consumed
in that overwhelming existence. For beauty is nothing
but the beginning of terror, which we are still just able to endure,
and we are so awed because it serenely disdains
to annihilate us. Every angel is terrifying,
And so I hold myself back and swallow the call-note
of my dark sobbing. Ah, whom can we ever turn to
in our need? Not angels, not humans,
and already the knowing animals are aware
that we are not really at home in
our interpreted world. Perhaps there remains for us
some tree on a hillside, which every day we can take
into our vision; there remains for us yesterday's street
and the loyalty of a habit so much at ease—
when it stayed with us that it moved in and never left.
Oh and night: there is night, when a wind full of infinite space
gnaws at our faces. Whom would it not remain for—that longed-after,
mildly disillusioning presence, which the solitary heart
so painfully meets. Is it any less difficult for lovers?
But they keep on using each other to hide their own fate.
Don't you know yet? Fling the emptiness out of your arms
into the spaces we breathe; perhaps the birds
will feel the expanded air with more passionate flying.

When I had recited the whole of the First Elegy in English, I attempted to read it out loud in German:

Wer, wenn ich schriee, hörte mich denn aus der Engel
Ordnungen? …

I had no German, and trying to read aloud in a foreign language was like munching strange and exotic fruit. Often I had to raise my voice, competing against the roar of the aggressive sea. We conducted an exhilarating dialogue. When we finished, those words mixed with the sounds of the sea continued to resonate in my head. It was then I decided that I would make a ritual to commune with the sea every morning. What a way to start the day! One Elegy each morning. My friend Ranier Maria would be happy.

I sat down on the rock, flat as a table, and watched the sea swell, heave, sway. The sun rose gradually behind me, after having cleared the upper rim of the mountains. I felt its warmth on my back.

Soon it got too hot. I rose and made my way back to the cottage. It was time for lunch. I opened a can of sardines and ate this with slices of buttered bread. After a cup of coffee and a cigarette, I went into the bedroom and brought out a Penguin copy of *Oblomov* by Goncharov. Book in hand, I reclined on the sofa and began to read.

I will always be grateful to Penguin. Without this indispensable publisher, my education would have been poorer and narrower. Not only were their books affordable to the shallow pockets of students, but their lists were reliably selective. I had already begun collecting literature: Conrad and Gide, Stendhal and Faulkner; and not only the classics, but good contemporary writing as well, Waugh and Nabokov. And not just literature, for my reading had extended to philosophy, politics, history and economics.

It was always a joy to browse through a shelf of those great little books with their plain covers. I would not have benefited from the "University of Penguins" had it not been possible to own a Penguin book for less than the cost of a simple meal.

The copy of *Oblomov* was a second-hand Penguin I had bought for two shillings from a bookshop in College Street in Dublin. The print was tiny, the leaves had turned slightly yellow with age, but I was immediately transported to 19th-century Russia. Periodically, like the book's hero, I was overcome by sleep and dozed off on that quiet afternoon in the country.

When I woke from these small naps, it would take me a few moments to reorientate. I would be struck with wonder that I was in a small cottage in Connemara, spending an afternoon reading a great Russian novel. My home in Malaya seemed very far away. Every once in a while, the improbability would strike me. How did I get here? What relationship did this have with the past? Where had I come from? Where am I going?

I later learnt this to be the affliction of the wanderer and wayfarer, the pilgrim, amazed at the road traversed and filled with wonderment.

I got up to get a drink of water. Aqua natura, H_2O, aqua miraculosa. Yes, the miracle of water! I felt the cold coursing down my gullet to reach the *dan tien*, the field of elixir in the Chinese traditional art of *qi kong*, situated two fingers' width below the navel. I returned to the sofa and *Oblomov*.

I lost myself in the book again. What was taking place in the novel became more vivid and real than my surroundings. Once in awhile, my eyes would dart to the window and the sunlit sky outside. The summer afternoon beckoned but it was only when my eyes grew tired and the printed page became hazy that I put the book down and stumbled out into the sunlight. The glare at first was dazzling, a million, brilliant flashing knives. I shielded my eyes with my hands.

Although there were a couple more hours of sunlight left to the day, I dismissed any inclination to wander beyond the area around the cottage. I had been too restless of late. Always on the go, doing this, doing that, in constant fear of missing something. Now I wanted to stay still awhile.

Teach us to care and not to care
Teach us to stay still

So I paced the grounds, taking slow, deep breaths. I sat down on a soft grassy spot facing the sky and the sea and smelled sun-baked grass. The sky's blue spaciousness forecast a coming night of stars. At the edge of the land, the sea heaved and sighed. Time slowed.

Later, I went in to fetch a beer, then returned to the same spot. In a cloudless sky, the sun sank, without hesitation or doubt. God of life, God of heat and light. I watched the glittering ball and the ever-changing colours of the afterglow sink below the dark ocean. I stayed till night was fully installed.

Inside, I made a peat fire and cooked dinner. I did everything without hurry, with full deliberation; the performance of the dance was its own justification.

Again, I had good appetite, but I ate slowly, enjoying each mouthful. The quiet, the light of the peat fire flickering on the moon-white walls, fell on me like a benediction. Afterwards, I washed up the few plates and cups, and went to lie down on the sofa. I lit a cigarette and poured out a good glass of poteen. Later that night, I read *Oblomov* in bed. The night felt safe. Nothing threatened.

As a child, in the dark protean, tropical nights, with their fecundity of life and death, rot and decay, everything was threatening. I was terrified of child-eating monsters and used to sleep with my scout knife beside my pillow.

Whereas tonight, alone in the Connemara countryside, in the pitch darkness, I felt serene. Before long, I fell asleep. I woke just before dawn from pleasant, irretrievable dreams. I pulled on a sweater, wrapped myself with a blanket like a Mexican serape and ventured out. It was dark. Above, a new moon, and brilliant concoctions of stars in their endless, stellar choreography, which had a potent effect on me. Not sure whether I felt diminished or magnified, I lingered awhile in the open night, taking in and absorbing. I became part of it as it became part of me, all sadness mixed with enchantment and almost painful lucidity.

Like an apparition of God, the sun rose progressively from behind the mountains bearing light, bringing life. All now revealed, I returned to the cottage, to bed and slept. When I reawakened, the day fully entrenched and claimed by my myriad companions on earth, I performed my morning ablutions in spring water. After breakfast, I went down to the sea, carrying Rilke. The waves dashed against the rocky shore, creating sound and fury, which still awed and frightened. The relentlessness of the sea. At the appropriate hour, in this place, I recited aloud the Second Elegy:

... But if the archangel now, perilous, from behind the stars
took even one step down toward us: our own heart, beating
higher and higher, would beat us to death. Who are you? ...

... Lovers, if they knew how, might utter strange, marvelous
words in the night air. For it seems that everything
hides us. Look: trees do exist; the houses
that we live in still stand. We alone
fly past all things, as fugitive as the wind.
And all things conspire to keep silent about us, half
out of shame perhaps, half as unutterable hope ...

The configuration of the day remained unchanged from yesterday's. I did the same things; made breakfast, ate it, made lunch, ate it too, sat looking at sky and sea, read and then took a nap in the afternoon, had tea, wrote in my journal, looked at the sky and sea, read, prepared dinner and ate it, sat, read *Oblomov* and so forth. In all these actions, there was intention and deliberation, establishment of routine, of pattern. Now, no longer from restlessness, from wanting to work. Rather, from a realization that quotidian life was circuitous, one day more or less the same as another. Could I learn to bear this, to live like this? And without despair? Could I endure the unchangingness of each day? The Beckettian sentence?

So I carried on doing the same things, breathed, ate, pissed, shat. And one day passed, then another, then the third day, the Third Elegy, shouted at the place where the sea met the shore, the waves in constant agitation — surprised the rocky shore was still there, it should have been in smithereens by now:

... But inside: who could ward off,
who could divert, the floods of origin inside him?
Ah, there was no trace of caution in that sleeper; sleeping,
yes but dreaming, but flushed with what fevers: how he threw himself in.
All at once new, trembling, how he was caught up
and entangled in the spreading tendrils of inner event
already twined into patterns, into strangling undergrowth, prowling
bestial shapes. How he submitted—. Loved.

Loved his interior world, his interior wilderness,
that primal forest inside him, where among decayed treetrunks
his heart stood, light-green. Loved. Left it, went through
his own roots and out, into the powerful source
where his little birth had already been outlived. Loving,
he waded down into more ancient blood, to ravines
where Horror lay, still glutted with his fathers. And every
Terror knew him, winked at him like an accomplice ...

So the day passed, only to be replaced by another. Each day spent in a similar fashion, during which I had not gone beyond the cottage grounds. Three or four days gone, not a trace left. Somehow, they had slipped away in a flow that swept me along. Yet, to live, I could do worse. Only, I agreed, as in the Fourth Elegy, which I roared at the sea, a leonine roar:

... And not refuse to go on living ...

Then the idea came to explore the shore that lay beyond the cottage. After breakfast, I packed provisions for the outdoor adventure and set out. I made my way north through hills and scrub vegetation. I did not encounter anyone, only sheep grazing on the grass, green here and there, otherwise barren and rocky. A number of sheep were feeding with heads bent and ignored me, while others raised their heads at my approach, eyeing me warily. It was quiet save for the bleating of sheep and the sound of the sea.

The shoreline led north. The sun mounted the sky. I was working up a sweat. I pressed on. The physiognomy of the terrain began to change. The hills flattened out, the shore became less rocky, and when I came round a bend, a long, sandy strand stretched out before me. Fine, white sand replaced the jagged black rocks. The beautiful beach was deserted. It was all for me.

I sat on the sand, doodling with a finger, regarding the scenery. I removed my shoes and felt the fine sand trickle between my toes. The sea gently kissed the shore, could not give enough kisses, it seemed. A white gull crossed the sky in front, barely flapping its wings, riding the air.

The setting was idyllic, serendipitous. I felt lucky to be located there in that spot, that time, to be alive.

The day burnt still brighter. Light reflected from the fine, desiccated grains of sand. I entered into the full heart of noon. I headed for some sand dunes beyond the headland. When I got there, I found a small cemetery by the sea. At once, I associated it with Valéry's:

Ce toit tranquille où marchent des colombes,
Entre les pins palpite, entre les tombes;
Midi le juste y compose de feux
La mer, la mer, toujours recommencée
Ô récompense après une pensée
Qu'un long regard sur le calme des dieux!

There were no more than a couple of dozen tombstones planted on the slight rise of ground. Many were grouped together, perhaps enfolded within a family site, while the single stones, singularly lonesome to the very end, stood on tiny platforms. The simple headstones with their chiselled names and dates, as if on roll call, were white and clean, bleached by the sun and washed by the rain. Tussocks of tall grass fought for space, mocked by the unblemished blue amplitude of sky above. Underneath the earth lay the dead, their bones picked clean by maggots, their bodily fluids absorbed by the unsaturated earth. Yes, there they lay in their uniform simplicity, abidingness now.

I felt when my time came, as indeed it must, I would like to be interred in such a spot under the common sky.

That afternoon, at the cemetery by the sea, I felt like a poet! I felt equal to it. I understood that to make a poem, I must enter into a state of innocence.

❦

To break the chronological structure of this account, I wish to jump ahead to another occasion some two years hence. Again I was in Cloch na Rón, this time with George Campbell and his wife Anna, both close friends of the Trimbles. George was a fine painter as well as an accomplished flamenco guitarist. At that time, the Campbells were spending half a year in Spain, and the other half in Ireland, with forays to London on business.

I admired the looseness of their lives, their juggling of time and space, their sense of control. I resolved to emulate them one day. I imagined straddling worlds, like the death-defying stunts of a high-wire walker or trapeze artist as he flies above the crowd.

I had taken to George the moment we met. He was totally unlike the stereotype of the artist. George was short and stocky, with a gentle softening and swelling to his girth, on the way to a beer belly. His sleek, thinning hair was a brilliantined mousy-black. He affected a wicked theatrical goatee.

George and his guitar were inseparable. He held it like a husband guarding his wife; his real wife Anna did not receive the same treatment and concern. In contrast to the curves and contours of his musical instrument, Anna was excessively thin and pale.

I admired George's paintings, his use of colours, his successful straddling of the representational and the abstract. We always enjoyed each other's company and shared a passion for literature and wine.

I brought George to the cemetery by the sea during that visit. He sat about surveying the scene, sometimes sitting in still concentration, sometimes caressing a headstone with painterly fingertips. For a long while, we did not speak.

Back in Dublin some weeks later, George telephoned and said that there was something he wanted to me to see. I went across to his flat and was shown a large oil painting of the cemetery by the sea. It was beautiful and poetic. He had captured the essence of the cemetery. A lovely, lovely work. He said it was a gift for me.

I was touched by his friendship and magnanimity. The Campbells depended on sales of his artwork to live. It was a hard existence. The painting was too valuable and I could not accept it. I told George that I did not need it as the cemetery was already an integral part of me. I suggested that he keep it for himself. George countered that he did not need it also for the same reason. I do not know who has the painting now, but I like the notion that it might have been passed from hand to hand by people who did not need the painting after they had got to know the cemetery.

One night, we were sitting outside the cottage, the whole countryside drenched in moonlight, silvery and white, when George brought out his guitar and sang the deep song, the *cante jondo*. This music sprang from the soul-blood, the land and the people, of the gypsies of Spain — their fierce passion in the songs and dances. I watched George's fingers love the guitar strings and then his voice was unleashed in song, released bowel-deep, from within the ribcage, the brilliant red blood chambers of the heart and regenerative marrow in the bones, the percussive skull. Chanting and wailing in concert with life and death, and always, always, a mix of suffering and joy, suffering and joy.

Noontime, and shadows retreated to their sources. White sky, blue sea, glittering sand. The moment when the nimble spirits hatch from under the tombstones as if from gigantic eggs incubating in hot sand, roosted over by the sun. They scurried about in the heat.

I unpacked my lunch and invited them to a picnic on the grass, *un déjeuner sur l'herbe*. We were a little formal with one another for we had not been properly introduced; I had barely been able to read their faded names on the headstones. Moreover, they were not much interested in food. I sensed restlessness. Now and then, they would leap up, make elliptical trips among the feathery clouds, the whooping hardly contained as they swirled. After a while, after missing a whole bag of hints, I realized what they were after, what they had long been starving for, to engage me in debating philosophical puzzles. But I had no inclination for this, nothing beyond sharing a picnic on the sand. I had no wish to be quarrelsome. It would be tiresome to argue over abstractions on such a fine day!

As expected, there was sulking and I packed up early, called it a day.

As I left, turning around the bend at the end of the strand, the sea was still laughing, in that long-shadowed, late afternoon.

ॐ

On the sixth day, I walked down to the large boulder early in the morning and howled the Sixth Elegy to the sea. I had not spoken to or seen another soul for six days and the constant interior monologue was making me claustrophobic. It was difficult to be a recluse, with no one to talk to. I wanted to break out of this cloister. Also, I needed provisions.

After breakfast, I set out for Cloch na Rón. It promised to be a fine day. No one was in sight and I had the road to myself. I had walked for about an hour when suddenly I heard a voice yell out.

"Helloo!"

I looked about and saw a man leaning on a stave down by the bog.

"Helloo, young fella!" he hailed again.

Lamely, I replied, "Hello."

"My son, could ya give an old man a hand, I wonder?"

Although he was some distance away, I could hear his every word distinctly.

"What can I do for you?"

"Could ya come down here a minute?" he beckoned with his hand.

I clambered down from the road to the flat field of peat. The man was in his sixties, tall and big-boned, with a large head sitting precariously on a long body. His face bore fine fingerprints, hinting of a tough physical life, and was as weather-beaten as the rocks around the fields. But all was offset by his blue eyes, liquid with merriment and mischief.

A two-day stubble sprouted from his upper lip. He offered a wide smile, ushered from a mouth filled with tobacco-stained teeth. I saw that he had a cigarette in his hand.

"Hi ya, young fella!" he greeted cheerily.

"Hello, how can I be of help?"

"Ah ha! You see this pile of peat I've cut? You see that shed over yonder?" he pointed with a thick sausage of a finger. "Well then," he continued, "I've to haul them cut blocks over for storage to that shed. Can ya give an old man a helping hand? It will take only a short while with a strong, strapping lad like yourself helping out." He beamed at me and waited.

"Sure, be glad to."

The blocks of fresh cut peat were each the size of a brick. We set to work, each filling a brown burlap sack with the bricks. Then tottered unsteadily with this burden towards the shed which was about 50 yards away. It was heavy going. The old man had a limp. Despite this, he did as much work as I did, a grin hovering on his lips. We did not speak, concentrating on our task. After a dozen trips, we paused to rest. It was hot. We took off our shirts. The summer sun rose to its zenith. Nothing stirred, no shady trees under which we might shelter, no sweet cordial wind to soothe our bodies. We stood there, squirming in the glare.

"What's your name, young fella? Me, they call me Paddy."

"Tony." I offered him my Christian name.

"You from the big city? From Galway?"

"Yes, I'm from the big city. But I'm from Dublin, not Galway."

"Dublin? Sure you come a long ways away. I meself have never been there, never set foot on it. Why, even Galway, I've been only a couple of times."

Yes, definitely tethered to his own place on earth. While I, I had become a peripatetic traveller, footloose.

"Now, if you don't mind," Paddy said, "let's carry on with our work," he urged.

So we began again to load the sacks of peat bricks and carry them to the shed. We were soon bathed in sweat. We halted again for another breather. The heat and stillness were intolerable. Oh for a cool breeze, a breeze, a kingdom for a breeze!

"No, I have never been to Dublin," he said, answering a question which I had not asked. "Too far away, I am not drawn to places too far away. Also, I don't care much for towns and cities neither. Too many people, if you ask me. I hated Galway city. Big crowds, big noise. I never understand how people can live like that. I would go stark crazy if I lingered more than a day there. No sir, I don't want to live in a city."

"You'd get used to it in time."

"I want none of it."

"Aren't you curious about the outside world?"

"Frankly speaking, no! I have no great interest in the outside world. They've nothing to do with me, and I've nothing to do with them."

"But we are all one big world!"

"No sir. Not one world. And I don't bother with what's nothin' to do with me. Too many busybodies bothering about everyone else's business, that's really what's wrong with the world today. I just mind me own business, that's all I want to do, leave others alone. All this here," he announced, sweeping grandly with his hand, "is my world! There's only one lifetime a man has, enough maybe for him to get to know his little bit of the world if he be lucky, if he be blessed, God willin'," and Paddy crossed himself.

He looked up at the sky, tilting his large head backwards. There, we saw crystallized in the bright light, a plane high up, skating gracefully across the white sky.

"That'd be the 12.05 flight out of Shannon, bound for Boston."

We watched it pass a moment, its drone coming from far away. Boston. Faraway places with those strange-sounding names, but what has that to do with us, who are standing on this flat bog, earth-bound and bounded by the chains of time. The sight made me marvel at the technology of man. Products of daydreams and fantasies, improbable, farfetched, absurd.

On that day, the two of us were stranded in time, on that hot shadowless afternoon, there was no hiding place, and none at all for secrets. Under that transparency, we could only construct speech out of veracity and clarity. Paddy, the man who truly belongs, was never ill at ease, and always plain in his utterances.

"Are you married, young fella?" he asked directly, pushing out his square jaw.

"No, I am not!"

"Good for ye! Never get married, young fella, never get married," he admonished loudly to make sure I got his message.

"Are you married yourself, Paddy?"

"Me?" he pointed a finger at his own chest. "Married? Never! Never!" he barked.

"Why is that so? There must be plenty of beautiful women in the village," I teased.

"Why? I'll tell you why! You see that hill over there?" He pointed. "There, on the leeside of it is me cottage. I have a field, a calf and a milch cow, which is generous with the best of white milk in the world. I have most things I need. The rest is greed. Living alone, I need very little."

"Are you not lonely?"

"Never!" he asserted. Then, as if he had understood my overloaded question, laughed forthrightly and added, "And I can still get me a woman. There are a few who are always willin'. Now, to return to me tale. One terrible day last winter, with hailstones and a lashing wind, the hailstones large as marbles, a part of the thatch roof flew away. Oh, it went sailing in the wind like the Devil himself had willed it. The damaged roof began to leak, right over me bed. Rainwater poured down as from a hole in the sky itself. So, what did I do?"

"Well, what did you do, Paddy?"

"What did I do?" He paused for effect, before recounting, "What did I do, me son? What I did do was I shifted me bed from the leaking spot. That way, the rain no longer fell on me bed." He waited for my appreciative laughter, then continued. "Now if I was married, I could not have done that could I? You can expect me wife pushing me and nagging me to mend the roof. Why, a man would have no peace at all until he fixes the blooming roof. Am I right or not right, young fella?"

I nodded my agreement with a laugh.

"A man will have no peace with a woman in the house, ruling the roost. Now, I admit, there are some men who would not have minded that, but yes, me son, I sure would mind that! I could not give away peace in me own home to a woman! Mark me words, if you want peace in your own home, young fella, never marry! Never, never!"

We returned to the task at hand. It soon transpired that I was fated to labour for Paddy that day. I put in some three hours of strenuous exertion which was never my intention. In the end, I stayed the course until the whole blooming pile of peat had been transferred to the shed. I was sore all over but it was never dull with Paddy regaling me with tall tales and gossip, fleshing out the landscape of the good souls who lived around Cloch na Rón.

We finally parted company when our shadows had shrunken to the size of a football. Heading for the village, I dribbled the ball.

During the next few weeks, I encountered Paddy whenever I went to the village. Each time we would stop and talk. Conversations with Paddy were not discontinuous. Although there were gaps in time, his words fell into place like irregular pieces of a jigsaw.

Apart from cutting and selling peat, he took good care of his milch cow and calf. He was also an odd-jobs man and part-time postman for the village. I often saw him limping his way out of Cloch na Rón with a canvas bag of mail slung across his shoulders.

We became good friends. And yes, I did help Paddy one more time with the peat.

೫

Gradually, I gained more familiarity with the landscape and some of the inhabitants. I appreciated the ever-changing hues of the hills, switching from grey to green, to bleached indigo to gold, varying almost from instant to instant. And the sea changed from black to glittering silver, and from blue to green. I noted the rocks by the shore, polished smooth by the sea-blast. I watched the clouds combed by the wind into white sculptures in the sky, and observed how the shadows of the clouds raked across the open fields and the sea's surface, and along the sides and peaks of the hills. The rich fields of grass, and the potato patches with their boundaries of hand-piled stones, brought a palimpsest effect to this land-scape of western Connemara, shadows falling on previous shadows, a shade added to bygone layers of shade. A consciousness lain on other consciousnesses that had existed earlier, displaying the affinities between the past and the present. There was crafting and merging. All the while, time nibbled away at everything.

One afternoon, verging on twilight, the wind, a palpable presence, pushed against me as I stood on the small road sloping down to the stone jetty. I watched the curraghs riding the evening swell as the boatmen from the adjourning islands, silhouettes of blue dreams in the distance, head for Cloch na Rón and the mainland. Some of the boats were diminutive near the horizon, moving motes or insects upon the vast skin of grey water. Here and there was a curragh closer by, and I could see the men manipulating the long, wooden oars with dexterity and artistry. As I stood there a spectator, one by one, the curraghs beached and were tied up along the jetty. Once the boats were secured, the island men, a gaunt silent race, climbed up the small street and headed for the pubs, arriving exactly at opening time.

Daylight had begun to ebb as I dragged my body, leaning into a strong breeze along the coastal road back to the cottage. The moist evening air made the landscape mysterious, the fields exhaled a smell of fresh wet, of night dew. I walked past a few small stone houses, tightly shut, the faint light within harbouring domesticity. Home and family. That glimmer of home accentuated a growing loneliness I felt. In bed that night, I lay listening to the singing of the wind, disembodied voices floating up from the earth and the fields of grass, up to become tangled in the overhead electric wires strung alongside the road, bringing energy, invisible and incredible, to distribute heat and light to the cottages. The voices of the wind crashed into the leaves of the bushes. The moaning was nightlong, for whatever it was they were hankering for. And I was sucked into it, into moaning, moaning with desires, for what I did not know. Reclining, a lumpen pile on the bed, head stone-heavy upon the white pillow, heartbeats striving for synchronicity with the wind. It was not easy and I could not sleep. I tossed and turned, felt trapped in the interminable night. But dawn did break through, and I was still there.

❧

Later that afternoon, while taking my siesta, I heard loud, resolute knocks on the door. *Knock! Knock! Knock!* A pause. Then, *Knock! Knock! Knock!* Again, with determination. A rude interruption of my nap. I stumbled out of bed, all in a pile, and went to open the door. A young woman in a big, brown duffel coat smiled at me. She had a shock of reddish-brown hair and freckles on her face. She wore no make-up.

"Hi! I am Maryanne O'Neal. You must be Poh Seng," she said, thrusting out her hand to shake mine. Her fingers were short and stumpy, and bore nicotine stains. Her grip was strong and firm, hinting of manual labour.

"Hello!" I greeted.

"Joan and Garry invited me to come out here. We're to share the cottage. Hope you don't mind."

"Not at all!" I declared. "Please come in."

She entered, unloaded a big backpack and the portable easel attached to it.

"So you are an artist," I said.

"Yes, I am." She spoke with directness, without apology or arrogance. She remarked, "And I've been told that you are a poet!"

Touché! I thought.

"How are Joan and Garry?"

"They're both fine. And they send their love."

"Make yourself comfortable, Maryanne. I'll make some tea, then I'll clean out the bedroom for you."

"Thanks, I'll do it myself. I'm very simple, don't like fuss." She removed the heavy brown duffel coat, a curious garment to wear in midsummer. How could she bear the heat? She had on a pair of faded light-blue Levis and a sleeveless green T-shirt with damp spots at the armpits. Then I noticed the bushes of red hair sprouting there. All the women I knew had shaven armpits, which looked like the plucked backsides of chickens, with short stumps of hair. I found Maryanne's flaming red armpit hair sexually exciting.

I showed Maryanne to her room and then went to the kitchen to make tea. We sat at the small square wooden table.

"How long have you been here?"

"About three weeks," I replied. Yes, I had been there almost three weeks. I had completed my daily recital each morning of the *Duino Elegies*, shouting to the elements down by the sea. This circumscribed period of time constituted the only reality; my life before that seemed an invention, existed only in the land of fancy.

"Hope my coming here unannounced won't complicate the rest of your stay. You'll find me an independent person. I am used to doing my own thing. I don't need looking after."

"There should be no problem. Having company will be a nice change."

There was a certain lilt in her speech that was fresh and appealing.

"Are you American, Maryanne?"

"Yup! Massachusetts, New England. My dad came from Ireland, from Kerry. He runs a pub in Boston."

In return, I told her about myself.

"Are you staying long in Ireland, Maryanne?"

"I'm here visiting my ancestral home. The ould sod, ya know? But I have no firm plans really. Just drifting along. Paint if I feel like it. It's a pleasure trip actually," her words rippling along like a little stream.

"You'll find Ireland inspiring."

"Perhaps. But I'll take it real easy."

After tea, I showed her around, down to where the waves crashed against the rocks.

"Not much good for swimming, is it?"

"Not much good here. There are spots along the coast that are ideal. Long lovely strands without a soul in sight," I said encouragingly.

"Great! You can take me to them."

I promised to do so.

The afternoon advanced. We sat on a patch of grass, sharing smokes and a couple of cups of hot tea. Maryanne had brought a carton of Camels. At that time, I was an indifferent, or more correctly, an indiscriminate smoker. I could smoke and enjoy it, or stop and hardly miss it. I switched from cigarettes to a pipe to cigars. Those were the days before the cancer scare. Smoking was generally accepted, not considered an antisocial act. People used to smoke in the cinemas, and I remember the dense clouds of grey smoke hovering over the audience, which became for me, a part of the ambience of going to the films. There was the odd, staccato smoker's cough punctuating the dark, and red eyes stumbling out after the show, and one's throat tickled and irritated. It was all part of the allure, the romance of going to the cinema with a girl, holding hands, and necking in the dark under the clouds of smoke.

"Oh, I wish I could go for a swim," Maryanne sighed. "Or stand under a cold shower. I feel so tacky after the trip. All that dust and sweat."

"You can bathe in the stream. Water's clear and cold," I volunteered.

"Thanks! I'll do just that!"

"Have your bath. I'll prepare dinner. I am making a lamb stew."

"Look forward to it. I must admit I'm famished."

When Maryanne returned, wrapped in a big, colourful towel, her wet hair had turned a darker red. Her fair skin was spotted with freckles. She crossed to her bedroom. "Smells yummy," she declared.

About half an hour later, I lifted the lid off the pot. The stew was simmering happily. Maryanne had changed into clean clothes and pulled a chair into the kitchen to join me. She lit a Camel, then poured out a good measure of Bushmills into two tumblers and handed one to me. We lifted the glasses and toasted Ireland. The whiskey went down smoothly.

We sat down to eat, dipping torn chunks of brown bread to soak up the rich gravy. We dined by the light of a pair of red candles stuck into the necks of emptied Chianti bottles. These Chianti bottles with a distinct wrapping of woven raffia around their bases were popular decorative items in the fifties and could be seen in almost every student flat or room. The candlelight softened the night as we talked.

Maryanne's paternal grandfather had left county Kerry for America when he was 18. He worked as a labourer for several years up along the east coast of the United States, and married an Irishwoman, also a new arrival from Kerry. They settled in Boston where he got a job as a teamster in the docks. Needless to say, it was a hard life for the young couple. Maryanne's grandmother worked for many years in a packaging plant to supplement the family income. From the beginning, they were discriminated against by the English, who had settled in the new country earlier. The prejudice suffered by the Irish immigrants was later perpetuated by them against other newcomers.

As the Teamsters became a powerful union, wresting improved wages and working conditions out of reluctant business owners, life improved for Maryanne's grandparents. Her grandfather managed to buy a house and send his children to school.

The next generation fared better. Together with two of his brothers, Maryanne's father operated three taverns and a popular bar restaurant. Three other brothers went into the professions and an aunt became a violinist with the Boston Symphony Orchestra. The true passions of the exuberant O'Neal family, however, were politics and racehorses. Maryanne had been unsure of what she wanted to do, but had drifted into the Arts, eventually enrolling in the Fine Arts College in Boston.

"I still really don't have a firm plan. I'm playing it all by ear," she admitted.

Her family history was much like my own. My grandparents emigrated from South China, and lived through the common story of hard work and exploitation, always striving for a dream, each generation making an advance. As for my own dream, I knew I wanted to write but was confused and clueless as to how I was going to become a writer.

"Is your family supportive of what you want to do, of your being an artist?" I asked.

"I'm very much my Daddy's girl, and can bank on his support no matter what I do. But I do believe that he's pleased, or at least curious about my passion for Art. I think that for him, coming from a background of hard labour, of overcoming practical obstacles, Art is a luxury, a commodity for the rich. It tickles his fancy. He might feel that this crazy, impractical quest of mine proves that his family had arrived. That a daughter can pursue such a useless and frivolous trade. It denotes a step up the social-cultural ladder. But what about you, do your folks support your dream?"

"Actually, I haven't broached the subject with them yet. My parents believe that I am pursuing my medical studies diligently."

"Aren't you close to your family?"

"Of course I am! I've not told them because I don't want them to worry, to be upset. Besides, the notion of being a writer is without precedence for people with my background, which makes it difficult to explain. There are no exemplars. Our lives are pragmatic, if not desperate. Our condition is that we are a colonized people, and culture has low priority for us. We are just a typical middle-class immigrant family, deculturalized and unsophisticated. I am the first one in the family to receive a tertiary education."

We chatted quietly, downing Bushmills and smoking Camels, cruising along with time. Then the rain came, knocking against the glass window panes, Mother Nature tapping at the window, sending us to sleep. We retired to our separate beds.

୧୫

The next morning, it was dull and grey, with clouds pressing down on the mountains, and every blade of grass seemed wet. It was Sunday and Maryanne wanted to go to Cloch na Rón to attend mass. So we set out early on foot. She packed a knapsack with materials for sketching and painting. I brought along a dog-eared notebook and Eliot's *Selected Poems*. As we walked, passing the grey eminences of hills to one side, and to the other, the ocean, washing along the rocky shore, we could smell the wet morning air, the freshness of the earth. A light wind spread the ghostly shadows of clouds across the whole landscape. We came upon a herd of horses grazing on the green hillside, and I told Maryanne they were wild Connemara ponies brought over from the Aran Islands. They had great strength but were very timid.

164

When we reached Cloch na Rón, it looked quite deserted. Most likely, the population had gathered in the churches. Maryanne and I made straight for Father Cassidy's church, just in time for mass. An air of piety hung over the interior, and we rose and knelt obediently together with the faithful congregation. Maryanne went up to receive Holy Communion. I watched her face when she returned, wrapped with the gift of grace; there was a directed inward focus as if she was truly filled with God. Yes, grace. Which is God within. Something holy. Something I lacked. I felt a conspicuous outsider, lonely and lost.

After mass, I brought Maryanne to meet Father Cassidy who was holding court with his parishioners by the front entrance. He asked us to visit him, perhaps for lunch after mass the following Sunday. We readily accepted this kind invitation. Then I formally introduced Maryanne to Paddy, who was dressed in his Sunday best like the other villagers. The entrance was jammed with people. Everyone donned clothes especially kept for this holy day of the week. It was part of the ritual of living in that community, a very old custom. There is a certain change in a person when he or she takes the trouble to dress up for mass. It gives a sense of occasion, heightens the significance of the event, and it is good to have a sense of occasion in a dull and drab life.

We found a small teashop and had a simple breakfast. Afterwards, we walked down to the jetty. It was so quiet along the promenade, I could hear the small waves below. Maryanne set up her materials and began to sketch the stony harbour. This attracted a bit of attention, and a few of the more curious onlookers approached her and stared with uplifted eyebrows while she worked. One does not usually come by an artist publicly toiling at her work in these parts. And what a queer thing to draw: the jetty. Their jetty which had been part of the village since they were born. That anyone could take the trouble to draw it. Queer indeed!

Watching, I found her a neat and fastidious worker, quite unlike her apparent disregard for how she looked. It was obvious she did not set much store on grooming, for she always dressed plainly, carelessly. There was her baggy duffel coat, not at all smart. Her wild head of hair, stained fingers, rough to the touch, and her dusty brown hiking shoes. It was as if she focussed her energy and attention on her work rather than on her person. She had set her priorities. Her art came first. I observed her as she took a short break, lighting a cigarette, and examining her handiwork critically. Maryanne pushed her way through the knot of men, exchanged a few words with one of the onlookers, an old man with long white hair and beard. A short while later, she detached herself and returned to her work.

I continued to idle about while Maryanne sketched. I never once opened my notebook or Eliot's poems. There was ample pleasure in doing nothing, being as simple as the gulls cruising above the water. When Maryanne was through, she packed her things away in her knapsack. She did not offer to show me her work and I did not ask.

"Well, I am ready for a drink," she declared with anticipation. It was late afternoon and a soporific air had descended on the village. I relished a drink but was a bit worried that a woman in these parts would be unwelcome in the public part of the pub. Usually, the women were escorted to a private room or a separate saloon if there was one. I explained this to Maryanne and as expected, she dismissed this fear as nonsense. She strolled resolutely into the pub and I followed with trepidation.

At once, the buzz of conversation stopped. In the pregnant silence, Maryanne pushed her way through the crowd of men, and headed for the long bar counter.

"Hi! Good afternoon!" she greeted each one as she passed and manufactured a beneficent smile at everyone. Nobody responded to her greeting. In time, she made it to the long bar with its multiple gleams of glasses and bottles.

"What can I get ye, son?" the bartender asked me, pointedly ignoring Maryanne.

"A pint of Guinness, please. What about you Maryanne?" My voice sounded inordinately loud in the quiet.

"A Jameson," she replied. Then Maryanne spoke out like a loud bell. "C'mon, name it boys. I am standing!"

Jesus, Mary and Joseph, I thought. Now she's done it! Her impudence had surely gone over the line. I knew there was an inflexible rule that he who stood a drink would be stood one in return. It was unlikely that a lone woman would be allowed to stand a round. I flushed with embarrassment. I knew the rough men of Connemara could be gallant, but they could also be hard and uncouth.

"You rich Americans think that you can buy anything!" someone said.

"Now hold yer flippin' fire, Mike. It's a lady you are speaking to!" a small old man standing in the corner said.

"What's wrong with you lot?" Maryanne exclaimed. "Me dad's Da is from Kerry, and me Da is a publican in Boston. I only wanted to make a toast," she declared, and then raised her glass of whisky and shouted "Here's to Connemara! God bless Connemara!"

Almost everyone in the house raised their glasses and shouted as a man, "To Connemara! God bless Connemara!"

"And here's to Ireland! May God bless Ireland!" Maryanne commanded, and the whole room followed her.

After that, the atmosphere became gay and animated. Maryanne was very popular. Everyone wanted to talk to her. To each one, she'd dip her hands into the sumptuous pockets of her duffel coat, fish out a sweet and offer, "Here, have a candy!"

She never seemed nervous or cautious. Her straightforward, candid, easygoing manner endeared her to everyone. They all loved her. I watched her, I must admit, with envy in my heart, knowing I could never be like Maryanne. I had been shy all my life, believing myself a sensitive soul. Or perhaps, it was arrogance? At any rate, there was a restraint, a kind of paralysis which often resulted in my forgoing a chance to forge another human relationship. Shyness is like a frigid landscape of the soul. This feigning of self-sufficiency, indifference, even of fear and cowardice, only put others off. But I knew what was inside of me, and I had resolved that I would not be shy or afraid in my writing. That knowledge or determination assuaged a little.

By the time we left, we'd both consumed quite a lot, and were more than a little drunk. There were friendly and warm farewells from our new friends. We walked back at an easy pace and in a bit of a trance. On the journey, a shaft of sunlight broke through the smudged sky, incandescent on every hill and field, on every cottage, stunning us with its beauty. It was an epiphany. We walked past a rustling brook, laughing without reason. We came upon a roan-coloured pony, raising its head, tossing its long mane like a flame in the wind, its coat a lovely sleek. He whinnied at us and I wanted to pat it, to caress with my hand.

As a consequence of the afternoon's drinking, we did not feel like cooking an elaborate dinner. We munched on bread and cheese, and went early to bed. I could not even read.

❧

We woke up to a sunny morning, the sky bright and clear, the sea still like glass, and decided it was as good a day as any for a swim. So, after breakfast, we packed towels and prepared a picnic lunch of cheese and bread, apples, and a bottle of white Italian wine of nondescript origin. Maryanne brought her sketchbook, and I, my notebook, an indispensable prop, but I harboured no great expectations or ambition for much work on a day like this. It was a day for enjoyment.

We made our way along the coast, passing several beaches, until we came upon a small, curved bay in the recesses of a pile of rocks, fairly close to the cemetery by the sea. And so, ghost-guarded. Sheltered, silent, no wind, sand bone-white. No other soul in sight. The dull green swell of water enticed like a lover.

"Christ! It's beautiful!" Maryanne exclaimed, "I'm going to skinny dip."

She deposited her belongings high up on the beach, and without hesitation, proceeded to take off her clothes until she was completely naked. She stayed there a moment, illuminated, the light gathered around her. I looked at her. I believed there was nothing more beautiful or more miraculous than the female human body. This was the first time I had seen one in my carnal innocence. There Maryanne stood, so naked and so true. Her breasts a joy, her private garden secret with short, dark tendrils of hair. She walked down to the sea and entered it. When she emerged and stood up in the shallows, her skin gleamed and was wet from the water falling lovingly down her white body. Aphrodite newly risen.

"Come join me," she entreated.

At once, I obeyed her command, and stripped off all my clothes. Although I had packed swimming trunks, I could not wear them. It had to be nakedness to nakedness. This was the first day for us in the Garden of Eden.

The air was cold and I was self-conscious walking down to the water. She watched me approaching and I felt exposed, afraid I would get an erection under her gaze. Fortunately, the first touch of the sharp sea cold disposed of this problem. My prick and balls instantly froze, turned shrunken and blue.

"It's cold!" I said.

"Yes, but once you plunge in, in a few moments you'll be fine."

We waded deeper into the water. She was the first to plunge in. The next moment, she rose out of the water, yelping joyously. Then I plunged in, and was at once numbed by the cold. It was unbearable, and I found it hard to breathe. After a while, I got used to it. We swam out together, bewitched by the sea's immeasurable surprises. Later, we stood in waist-high water, our feet resting on the coruscated sandy floor, a couple of feet apart. Her breasts were wet and delicious, her nipples coral pink. Through the water I saw a refraction of the lower portion of her body, but distorted, a wavering form like a big slithering fish. There was a vague suggestion of her hairy pubis.

We chatted awhile and then swam out again. Afterwards, we ran along the strand, her bosoms bouncing, whilst my limp cock flopped up and down with each stride, which made us laugh. Maryanne spread out a towel on the sand and sat down. I sat beside her. She leaned forward, resting her chin on her knees. Drops of seawater scattered like adornment on her body. She smelt of the sea. She laid down on the towel, stretching and unravelling, offering the feast of her nudity to the sky. Her eyes were closed as if in bliss. What beauty! My desire mounted. The only witnesses were the small birds flitting about in the sand. My thoughts too flitted about, my emotions jumping and skipping like the small birds.

Yet I made no move towards her, but turned supine, and felt my hardening cock rubbing against the rough texture of the towel. I shut my eyes, conscious of my breathing, of air sighing in and out. I felt the ticking of my heartbeat and lay still, silent as time. I wanted to act in praise of flesh, of life and passion. Instead, I lay inert, stiff and helpless.

When she turned over to lie on her stomach, I noticed a crop of freckles blemishing her upper back, which I found appealing. Her globular, full buttocks were ripe for the taking.

I was worried she might notice my erection. But she acted quite naturally, and the wholesomeness of that day stayed intact. This was the real world and I marvelled that we were there together. We swam and napped on the beach, the summer sun benevolent all the while. When the first fingers of wind touched us, we dressed and headed back, our world beneath the shadow of the mountains shifting into peace and silence.

The day stretched long and it was marvellous to be with Maryanne. Yet I felt unfulfilled, a maudlin, petty, comic grievance eating at my soul. All my life, I had been afraid of missing something, afraid of being short-changed. I had an insatiable appetite for life without which I felt I would not be able to write. To write, I must live fully and experience everything.

After dinner, we sat over the last of the whisky. The candlelight threw a soft aura around us but it seemed we could not be fully relaxed. A small tension charged between us. It would appear that our nudity had a strange and potent effect of enchantment mixed with sadness, and a sort of almost painful emptiness claimed me.

Afterwards, I lay for a spell in the darkness looking out of the window at the astringent stars outside, twinkling, twinkling in the hollowness, and for no good reason.

Then Maryanne slid into my bed and embraced me. She was naked and there was whisky on her breath. We kissed, her tongue imparted the sweetest flavour, and I was transported with joy.

"Take off your clothes. Oh, take off your clothes," she demanded urgently.

Our naked bodies came together with perfect fit. I felt her body with every pore of my skin, and the sense of completeness and sensuality almost made me die of contentment. We exchanged long, lingering kisses and our hands explored each other's bodies with reciprocal amazement and wonder and the sure instincts of the human animal's ecstasy. Above all there was the feeling that we could put ourselves in each other's care, and that, in spite of everything, we trusted each other.

Her mouth started nibbling, tickling across my face, and on to my neck, chest and belly, down to the sides of my thighs. I groaned with pleasure.

"Oh touch me, touch me here!" she cried, taking my hand and placing it between her parted thighs. She trembled at my touch and moaned with a subterranean sound, from the very depths. My fingers felt the smooth, soft flower of her cunt, slippery and tender with juice. One of my fingers slid easily into her vagina. Fascinated, I played with her, brushing against her pubic bush, that wiry turf. Lascivious, she swooned, became totally wanton. Her hands sought my cock, and wrapping her fingers gently around it, caressed the shaft. Mutually exciting each other, we thrashed about on the narrow bed as if possessed. Maryanne manipulated our bodies until she was lying on her back, with me on top of her. Her eyes were glazed, her head tilted backwards, her belly thrust outward to receive me. She cried, "Oh put it in me!" and with her hand guided my cock towards the entrance. Her cunt was all wet and ready, and with a push, I entered. I felt her muscles enveloping my rod in a sweet grip. It was unbelievably, indescribably good and ecstatic to be inside her. We stayed still to prolong the moment.

She implored, "Fuck me! Fuck me!"

I also felt the irresistible impulse to plunge and withdraw, plunge and withdraw. Supporting myself on my hands, I pumped into her again and again, my balls slapping audibly against her pubes, her thighs open like the pearly gates. I thrust harder and harder and faster and faster until a crescendo built up and I felt the impending explosion. For a second, I thought of withdrawing before I ejaculated, but it was so good that I didn't care anymore. With an urgent, final thrust, I climaxed. Maryanne continued to thrust upwards, and when my limp cock slipped out, she sought my hand and urged me to play with her until she climaxed. Her body tensed and thrashed as though in a fit. We pulled apart, panting from the exertion, as the charge of sex slowly ebbed. We lay side by side. I was conscious only of the galloping in my chest.

We glided slowly along the down-drift after sex. "Can you pass me a cigarette?" she said.

I padded on bare feet and gingerly steps to fetch the Camels and matches. I still felt shy and exposed, with my ridiculous limp and shrunken cock. We lit cigarettes. Oh the odour and taste of seared tobacco!

"Is this your first time?" Maryanne asked, blowing out a cloud of smoke.

"Yes. Can you tell?"

"Perhaps. I wasn't sure. You were good."

"Was I?" This wasn't her first I suspected, remembering the knowing way she had played with me.

"Yes, you were."

Perhaps she was just being polite.

Maryanne blew out another bolus of smoke, and turned to me. For a moment, her eyes gazed beyond me and the room into time and other lovers. I had just had my first fuck, an incandescent landmark in my life.

"I'd love a drink, but I think we've polished off the whisky," she said.

"We have some lager. That should also be good. Like one?"

"Sure."

I padded across the room, still self-conscious of my nakedness. We sat up in bed with our cigarettes and bottles of lager.

"Your first time! Are you disappointed?"

"No, no! Of course not. It was great!"

"Was it really up to expectation?"

"It exceeds it. The real thing is wonderful!"

"I'm glad. You didn't think I was too forward and improper?"

"'Course not! Why should I?"

"'Cause I'm a woman and you Asians are more formal and conservative."

"I don't think so. I'm no authority but I don't think we Asians are so uptight about sex."

"I'm relieved. It would pain me to feel you regard me as forward for making the first move."

"I'm happy you did."

"It's natural isn't it? It was such a lovely day and this felt right, inevitable. I'm glad we made love although we can't feign love, can we?" She looked at me.

I shook my head in agreement.

"Some people consider sex without love to be wrong. But I think anything that ecstatic must be good."

The truth of the matter was that all this talk was inappropriate. Trivial words after such an act!

After awhile, Maryanne ran out of words. And a certain coldness took hold of us, at first infinitesimal, but soon almost all encompassing and we began to feel awkward with each other. A case of post-coital distress, perhaps?

Suddenly, with a desperation, I turned to Maryanne and kissed her on the mouth, our tongues playing at lightning. Quickly, we were reinvigorated. This time, we made slow, lovely love, lavishly, lingeringly and the luxury of doing it without urgency. The rest of the night we slept the sleep of the sated, our bodies fulfilled, cradled by the warm summer darkness. The entire firmament in its proper place and all was harmony.

The next morning, I scrutinized her face and there was no hint of regret. It was only sex after all, the momentary physical union of two bodies, and life goes on.

In the weeks that followed, Maryanne and I were often happy. We made love daily. One night, I expressed a concern that we had not taken any precautions. I told her I had never bought a condom. It's her safe period, she assured me. Also, she used a diaphragm. She was so mundane about it, so practical.

Two days before her departure, we visited Cloch na Rón again. Once more, Maryanne sketched on the jetty and I mooned around. We spent some hours with the habitués of the pub, almost old friends now. Maryanne said her goodbyes, embracing everyone in sight.

The night before she left, we talked for a long time. Our separate futures. Maryanne mused about a long trip to Mexico, for the different sky, different earth, people and culture. Good for her. For me, the return to Dublin and my pursuits, although there were no firm expectations or anti-cipations. Life happens.

The next day, she left on the coach and I stood on the road, watching her go. I really wasn't unhappy. As I turned away, I was thinking what kind of second-rate love affair was this?

Before long, it was also time for me to leave. I spent an afternoon in Cloch na Rón, walking among the villagers. I scrutinized their faces, how the sea had used the old men, how the land had drained their strength. I said my goodbyes, and made my way back to the cottage.

Suddenly, from up the empty road, I caught sight of the familiar figure of Paddy, running and hobbling towards me, gesticulating wildly. As the old man drew nearer, I saw that he was in a state of great excitement. He ran right up to me, grabbed me by the collar and shouted:

"What's this that I heard in the village — that you are not an Irishman!"

I stared at him in amazement.

The old man tugged at my collar again:

"And what's this I hear — that the little blonde girlie is not your sister!"

I burst into laughter, caught Paddy by the arms, and the two of us danced a little jig down the road. Afterwards, we parted with a tight embrace. I felt the hard body right through to the bones of this old man whom I loved.

❧

The following morning, all packed, I locked the cottage and walked away. I looked around for the last time. It pained me to know that these days of summer were unrecoverable, indeed were already disintegrating, to be reconstituted into the past. The sky above was fluid with grief, the sea murmured farewell, and the mountains witnessed all.

But having lived through this summer at Cloch na Rón, I felt already that I would never die.

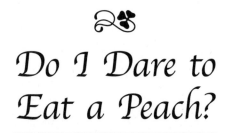

Do I Dare to Eat a Peach?

After a year in London, Goh Poh Seng returned to Dublin and completed his medical degree at UCD.

Do I dare to eat a peach?
I shall wear white flannel trousers, and walk upon the beach.
I have heard the mermaids singing, each to each.

I do not think that they will sing to me.

AFTER A LONG, DRAWN OUT winter, it was not easy for me to walk away from sunshine, however tentative and fragile. I was born and bred in the tropics so wilt like a flower in darkness when deprived of sunlight. For the duration of winter, I am driven to seek company, and what better place than the intentional intimacies of a pub?

One dark wintry evening, tired and listless after a day's attempt at studying, I felt I was not making much progress, my brain dull and stagnant as the massive clouds saturating the sky outside. I packed up my textbooks with exasperation and decided to seek some congenial company, and what better place than that of the intentional intimacies of a pub. I ended up at McDaid's.

Ah — the pubs of Dublin! I have travelled near and far, but seldom have I found a pub or bar to match the conviviality of the ones in the Dublin of my youth.

I spotted Sean Breslin across the room.

I had first met Sean a couple of months earlier, soon after he came to Dublin. All we knew of him then was that he was a young man with a gravity that belied his years. His air of formality made him appear a little aloof. Seated at a corner of McDaid's, he seemed quite contented to drink most of the night away. There was a certain quiet self-sufficiency about him that I liked. When he was still around after two weeks, our curiosity about him was justifiably piqued.

Who was this young man from Manchester? Sean was hard to categorize. He did not fit into any one of the usual modes. He was different from the usual, average fellow whom one comes upon in the easy atmosphere of a pub. He had piercing blue eyes, constantly animated, that seemed to bore into your soul, into the most secretive places of your being. That he was a non-conformist, all would agree. He wore his hair long when long hair was uncommon. His clothes also were not in keeping with the fashion of the day. He appeared to be wearing not his own clothes, but rather hand-me-downs from his father, and even his grandfather. He looked as if he had stepped in from another era, if not another world. He was always well-mannered and I suspected he aspired towards gravitas a little too obviously. I thought this un-belonging-ness marked him as an outsider, a character from one of Beckett's plays or novels. That, I must admit, was what interested me in him.

Sean seemed to have a lot of money. Several older regulars had commented on his generosity, that he did not mind buying drinks for others. Still, he remained an enigma. One sensed he did not come from a wealthy family. He did not have the demeanour of the rich, nor an accent inculcated at a public school. His background seemed to be quite modest. His shoes were those of a working man.

Then the mystery lifted. It transpired that Sean had inherited a fortune from a lost-lost uncle. He could not remember this uncle or what he looked like. A registered letter had reached him one morning from a solicitor in Manchester bearing the news that his uncle had passed away and left him the sum of £50,000. There was no message from the deceased of a personal nature, and no other instructions were contained therein. Upon investigation, he learnt that his benefactor was a younger brother of his father, who had gone into the contracting business somewhere in Kent.

Everyone at the pub congratulated him on his good fortune. A few boasted that they knew it had to be a big inheritance. They could tell that he was a young man of substance. The family's bearings in the man was so evident, and so on and so forth. Another chap, and his missus and his mother as well, spoke of the annals of the family Breslin, when, more than likely, no one in the family could spell the word "annals" or knew its meaning. It did not matter.

A couple warned him to be careful whom he made friends with: there were all sorts of sinners in this world. Alas, no one could be trusted. This opened up a voluminous discussion, indeed, discussions that lasted for weeks, on what this poor, rich young man should do with his money.

Even months later, people — mostly strangers visiting the pub, would sidle up to Sean, and give him an earful of advice on what he should do with his fortune. In a way, Sean became a famous man around Grafton Street. Sometime or other, someone would point a finger at him, sort of showing him off to a newcomer who was not one of the select few, not one of the privileged, who considered Sean a friend. In that vicinity, any man, woman or beast would be a celebrity if he, she or it, were worth 50,000 quid!

Sean had heard that I wrote poetry. He would not call himself a poet — not yet, he said. It did not sound like fake modesty. In fact, we were both in the same situation, frustratingly on the brink. Young then, I blamed it on the muse, whose visitations I eagerly awaited to no avail. Sean was likewise a fellow poet-to-be. Is there anything worse than this? We consoled ourselves with pints of Guinness, and soon became close friends.

He confessed, "I'm afraid fate has earmarked me to be a lifelong student: to only read and study the works of others. Oh so many others! One lifetime isn't enough, and yet is too much, much too much!" he cried, in despair. "To learn to write, I made up my stupid mind that I must digest and get to know the whole canon of English literature, no less. And not only the English, but also the Greeks, the Russians, the Germans ... You see my plight? And not only Literature, but also Philosophy. And not only that ..." he put his hands around his head as if to prevent it from bursting with knowledge, "but also Religion." After this recitation, he drained his glass.

"You're very ambitious," I said.

"You mean I'm mad!" he corrected.

"And how are you faring?"

"Can't you guess? Of course I'm doing abominably! Many people would say I'm complacent, that I'm lazy, sunk in lassitude, indulging in flights of fancy. They talk as if they know what it's like to be rich, to be one of those magical, enchanting creatures. Also, they believe the rich are capable of impossible actions."

"We're all jealous of you, never touched by poverty, a life of privilege, exempted from the daily grind, the ignobility of labour."

"Is that so? And what if I divulge to you that I've worked as a common construction labourer since I was 16? Here, examine my hands."

I took his hands in mine and felt the thick and rough skin over his palms and fingers. Strong hands, from long years of hard manual labour.

"I apologize. I'm totally convinced you're telling the truth."

"It may surprise you, but actually, my options are limited. My only experience is that of a labourer. Tends to run in my family, it seems."

"Are you at Trinity?"

"No, I wouldn't be able to pass the entrance."

"UCD?"

Sean simply shook his head. "I'm studying under some professors from the universities. I pay for private tuition. So I can choose the best."

He mentioned some names I was not familiar with. They taught in the Arts Faculty, whereas I was in Science.

Sean and I had the habit of always carrying two books with us, both of which we were currently reading. We often discussed the books, as well as those which had played an important role in our lives, or indeed had changed our lives. Sean was a keen collector of rare editions, and could indulge in it now that he had his inheritance. Whereas I had to restrict my purchases, and my limited library of fond books comprised those that were indispensable, which I read and reread. Revisited, they became close friends.

It was Sean who introduced me to *The Waste Land*, which he could recite in its entirety. He had an amazing list of poems that he had memorized, and I often requested a recital. He had a beautiful voice, a trait of his Celtic ancestry.

His appreciation of English Literature extended beyond the contemporary, into the eclectic. They stretched from Chaucer, his knowledge of whom almost made him a serious scholar, to Blake and Robbie Burns, Donne and Shakespeare. Nearer to our time, Whitman and Yeats, then Eliot and Wallace Stevens, Joyce and Beckett. He also loved Dylan Thomas. Of foreign literature, he knew the poetry of François Villon, Baudelaire, and Brecht. This list was far from exhaustive.

One afternoon in early Autumn, the trees beginning to change colours, the world transformed with a golden light, a season of mists and mellow fruitfulness, Sean and I were reclining on rented canvas chairs overlooking the small pond at St. Stephen's Green. We were inadequately dressed and there was a slight chill in the air: summer merging into Autumn, the change subtle and insidious, had come about without our noticing. So many things to contend with, the weather simply another topic.

"You should have come to see *Endgame* last night," Sean said.

"Yes. I've never seen a stage presentation of any of Beckett's plays. Guess I must make it a point to go."

So I went along that evening to the little theatre in Trinity College to see the production by the Trinity Players. The audience that night equalled the number of people on stage: viz., four. Disappointing to take all that trouble for such a minuscule attendance. But it was a riveting performance. I was totally absorbed in it. I laughed and cried, so moved was I.

During the interval, I went out to the tiny foyer for a cup of coffee. To my surprise, the cast came and joined us for refreshments. In costume and make-up, they were still very much the actors. This informality thinned the dividing line of the make-believe world of the stage from the one we inhabited.

The second act was equally good, and also brought me to laughter and tears. Afterwards, I left the theatre feeling drained yet elated, I wasn't sure which. Beckett's words resonated in my head. It was a profound epiphany — that I was a part of the same universe as the characters in *Endgame.* The communication with the play was almost holy, was full of grace, of the sharing of pain and happiness, of courage and laughter. And to laugh in the face of an absurd existence was nothing short of heroic. Yes, we are all heroes, simply just by being. As well, we are all under a death sentence, for which there is absolutely no reprieve. No, none whatsoever.

That late night, I could not sleep. Words and snippets from the play haunted me, went round and round my mind without let up and I was seized!

I returned to see the play again the next evening, and the evening after. It still held my interest and attention, and I laughed and cried as before. On the third night, at the interval, a young, bearded man came and introduced himself as the director of the play.

"You've been here nightly for the past three nights!"

"Yes, for the past three nights."

"We thought so. You arouse our curiosity. I hope you won't mind if I speak with candour."

"Yes, go ahead."

"That's pretty unusual, don't you think?"

"If you say so."

"Yes, pretty unusual. Three nightly performances in a row. Never before in my experience," the director continued, "have I encountered such emotional response, the crying, the desperate laughter, all on display. Pretty remarkable."

"Well, it's such a powerful performance of a great play. I felt it was wrong to hold oneself back. One must go all the way, to meet with the writer. And anyway, I usually laugh at tragedies, or so people have told me."

"That's pretty interesting," cried the pretty interesting director, as he came to be called in my mind.

"Listen, can you come on Saturday night, the end of our run? You see, the great man himself will be coming over from Paris for the closing. I would like to introduce you to Beckett."

"Thank you very much. I would like to come. Samuel Beckett is one of my real heroes. A great writer. He writes ... I was going to say — like an angel. But what I mean is that he writes like a 'man'. He is a man. He is one of us, all of us, living and dying, and perhaps even the dead. I'm truly excited!"

The following days, my mind was preoccupied by Beckett. I attempted to write him a poem. After many months and many drafts, I wrote "The Nothing New" and dedicated it to Beckett. It was a tribute from a young poet. It began:

nothing is new
all has turned to habit
i will not be
bewildered longer
by the nothing new

This poem was far from finished when I went to Trinity to meet Beckett that evening. He was just as I had imagined him: lean and wiry, with shots of white running through his dark, upstanding short hair like a parched field of grass. Deep furrows like crevices gouged his forehead. What terrain had his mind not ploughed? His eyes luminous like amethysts, or were amethysts luminous like Beckett's eyes? His eyes fixed on you with intensity, his voice beautiful as any described by J.M. Synge: a voice drunk in poetry, in words. Although the weather that singular evening was not cold, Beckett was dressed as though he were cold. He was in black with some touches of white. There was, to me, something of an unfrocked priest about him: this priest of words, prince of words, angel.

The young director said to Beckett, "This is the young Chinaman who laughed throughout your play!"

Silly bastard, I thought. Bound to be rebuked. Put on Oriental gentleman's inscrutable face to face the Master. Beckett stretched his hand out to shake mine.

"Well then, he is one who understands the play. I thank you," he said to me, kind as kind.

Later, as I made my way home, there was a melting in my soul like a florid sunset.

❧

That night, after mortal beings had been driven off the streets, I wandered about the silent, vacated cityscape, swooning within like one inebriated with a choice wine of very special vintage. I thought I heard the universe calling, enquiring whether I was a poet, not just a want-to-be, a wishy-washy dilettante. Wanting-to-be a poet is miles away from being one. Your proclamation after proclamation to all, as well as yourself, that you are a poet, is of no value. No, you're not a poet. You have produced nada, nothing, no good poetry to speak of. So how could you be a poet?

First, you use the excuse that you're still young, although Rimbaud had retired from poetry when he was 17! Yes, fella, retired, and at 17! He did so when he knew he had completed his oeuvre, his opus. While you, you haven't even started. You still have no oeuvre, no opus to speak of? You say you have to live life first before you can write, but what have you been doing if you have not been living all these 19, 20 years? You were existing, existing, replied ingenious you. Excuses, all excuses. You will not be a writer. You will never be a Samuel Beckett, a T.S. Eliot, a Joyce, a Dylan Thomas. You will be just you, a no-body. A plain non-poet.

So get off your fat arse and write poetry, if that's really what you want to do. No use groaning and moaning. So unbecoming. So shameful even. I looked up at the stars, those winking merciless scraps of the constellation, but they offered no guidance, no solace, none whatsoever. I walked about in a daze. I understood that this was a critical moment in my life — my long/short life, my existence. Yes, tonight's the night for decisions. It's Either/Or, says Schopenhauer.

For some time, I had realized things were coming to a head, but had tried to ignore it. I was torn. It was scary. It meant dropping my medical studies, which would be a great shock to my family. They had sacrificed so much to support me through medical school, and so much of their future depended on me earning a good income. I had to consider the university education of my siblings. My father was getting old and looking forward to his retirement. There was no chance of his pension stretching to support the education of the others. I dreaded to contemplate their reaction. They had been keenly anticipating my graduation and I had only slightly a year more of studies, after almost having completed five years! It didn't make sense to abandon medicine now! The whole prospect was tormenting. If anything happened to them, I would never be able to forgive myself. In my large extended family, as the oldest grandson, I had to set an example. It's difficult to explain this adequately to anyone.

On the other hand, I wanted to be a writer. I wanted to be fully involved in the life of writing, although the sensible course of action was to complete my studies. But then I would have to practise full time, leaving no time for writing. This was simply unacceptable, if I wanted to write seriously.

I remembered my English teacher at Blackrock College, Father De Vertuile, who was the first to steer me towards a life of literature. He had told me that a writer is so rare and important that he could be of more value to mankind than a thousand doctors. I had been thrilled and proud to be counted among the privileged coterie of writers. At that time, I had not had to consider the option of giving up medical school. Now I faced a no-win situation.

The key issue was whether I could write. Could I produce writing that was meaningful, that could give pleasure? I had not been writing seriously and the only way to find out was to give myself a chance. Give it a go. Take, say, a year to try it out. That option sounded feasible: I wouldn't have to burn my bridges, lose everything. My mind thus made up, I made an appointment to see the Dean of Medicine, Professor John Hamilton.

Going through the thin folder in which I kept my poems, there were very few I was satisfied with, much less felt proud about. Most seemed like dabbling. On this accounting, I wasn't confident that I was a poet. On these poems alone, there was little justification for me to take such a momentous step as to give up medicine. But an inner voice propelled me. I felt that my happiness depended on my decision.

I remembered those special weeks I had spent in Cloch na Rón. I had felt close to nature then, and close to writing. I seemed to be more distracted in Dublin, and the onerous programme one had to endure as a medical student was draining. There was no let up. Poetry and the creative juices just dried up. I regarded this paucity of actual writing as the consequence of my lifestyle, which went counter to what I call a life of inspiration. I had worked intermittently on a poem dedicated to Paddy at Cloch na Rón and another titled "Dublin Newsboy in the Snow", one of the few attempts which showed some sort of promise. These and two love poems to Hadley, lamenting lost love.

This small handful of poems was all that I had produced. If one was kind and encouraging, one could say, yes, there was some promise. But was that enough to justify my giving up medicine? There was little ground for optimism. The ice was thin and treacherous, and might in time split and crack suddenly, plunging the hapless skater into the depths.

But I was adamant that I should give up medicine. I recall speaking of this intention to Tom Pierre, who cautioned me not to be so impetuous and juvenile. He warned that I would regret this foolishness.

I also discussed my dilemma with Sean. He was delighted, and suggested that we go to Tangier — "Let's go to the Kasbah, Babee!" — and offered to finance the trip. Sean was irked when I turned this down. "It's the puritanical and bourgeois crap that you've learnt. Besides, I've decided to spend, spend, spend! I want to have fun, have what a great deal of money can buy." But I would not change my mind. Sean then decided that he would go with me to London, after I had formally dropped out.

❧

When I turned up at the Dean's office, Professor Hamilton kept me waiting. His very nice secretary, Miss Jean Moore bade me sit down as the Professor was running behind.

"I'm afraid I've only got an old copy of *The Lancet* for you to while away the time." *The Lancet* was the Medical Journal of The Royal College of Physicians in Britain. Miss Jean, as she was fondly called, was a small woman in her fifties known to be very helpful to students in trouble with the College. "And how are you getting on, Anthony?"

Miss Jean always addressed me as "Anthony", the name I had chosen when baptized a Catholic at Blackrock. I had got to know her well two years earlier when I had some problem with my attendance record and came to her for help. The university threatened to disallow those who fell short of the requisite attendance rate from taking the exams, and as a matter of fact, failed them. On that occasion, I had worn my best suit, the one made by Tom Pierre's Dublin tailor. (In measuring me, the tailor, Mr. Samuel, ascertained that my right shoulder was higher than my left. And ever since that day, I ascribed whatever ill health I had, to my abnormal, rogue right shoulder.) I turned up at Miss Jean's office with a small sprig of flowers, a cheap bouquet I'd bought at Henry Street on the way.

Miss Jean was delighted. "Is that for me? How sweet of you! I love these flowers."

When we came to the matter at hand, Miss Jean effected a grave face and, gently shaking her head, clucked her disapproval and concern. "This won't do, Anthony. They'll never let you sit for the exam. Look at all these empty spaces in your attendance card. You must get more of them filled. I mean you must get the relevant professors to sign them. If you do this, or rather, if they do this, then I'll just stamp them for you. But you better hurry, there's little time." That rubber stamp made Miss Jean a powerful figure in the school. So, over the next day or so, I became a master forger. Miss Jean then stamped my attendance cards, and I proceeded to the examination hall. And I passed the Third Year Pathology exam.

After that, I presented myself at my benefactor's office every year with a sprig of June flowers on her birthday. This was another brilliant and kind-hearted suggestion by Tom Pierre. It was he who found out about her birthday. How the old guardian angel beamed with happiness!

"Anthony, the Prof. will see you now!" and I was ushered into his office.

Professor John Hamilton was very much a man of the world, suave and erudite. He was regarded highly as something of a God by us lowly students. I had been looking forward to this meeting to expostulate my reasons for abandoning medicine.

"Yes?" he opened, after we had both sat down.

"Sir, I want to leave med school."

"That's good news."

"Sorry, sir. I don't understand. What's the good news?"

"You said you were leaving med school?"

I nodded my head.

"Well, that's the good news. If you're really leaving us. It's good riddance!"

I was incredulous! I had taken all this trouble and bother to personally come to explain my situation. I honestly thought he would try to persuade me to change my mind. Instead the bugger had taken a casual, almost hostile attitude. I was a bit dazed by this blunt answer. I had been expecting a quiet, civil, tea and sympathy sort of meeting. He must be pulling my leg. That's it! The Dean was playing the fool with me.

"You seem surprised. Let me assure you I'm most serious. I'll explain my attitude. Your assessment record, which I just looked at before you came, shows that your performance has been on the slippery slope, getting worse and worse. You did quite well in Pre-med and First Year med, and we thought you showed some promise. You were one of the better students. But something happened, and your downslide has been notable. In every aspect of your studies and training, you have put in a pathetic effort. Oh, you manage to pass all your exams, I vouchsafe that. For you're bright, and a token interest gets you through. You might even be able to graduate, but that will be gall to me. You will become one of those indifferent, slothful doctors who have no genuine interest in medicine. You will be a practitioner who short-changes patients and the community. So, I'm glad that you are leaving. Good riddance, I repeat!"

"Perhaps I lack the vocation to be a doctor. Then it's all to the good, don't you think, my departure?"

"But what a bloody waste! Someone else could have taken your place, who was excluded because you took his seat. You might not believe it, but it's a rare privilege to be a medical student. Your studies are subsidized by the Irish Government. That means that your tutoring, studies and training are paid for by every taxpayer among our citizenry. Don't forget that!"

"You make me feel bad."

"Yes. My intention is to make you feel bad."

"And you succeeded. Anyway I'm sorry. I feel chastened and guilty."

I was about to take my leave of the Dean, when curiosity got the better of him. He asked me why I wanted to give up medicine. The Dean had never met a student who gave up medicine voluntarily. So he was puzzled.

I told him my dilemma about being a doctor and a poet. Now, I said to him, at least that is resolved. He asked me what I had written. I told him that I had only a small handful of poems. He remarked that I was a brave man, then added that I was a romantic. I didn't argue.

We shook hands. The interview was over.

I was almost out of his office, when he said, "You can still change my mind. Last chance!"

I halted a moment, and then shook my head, rejecting his offer and walked away.

Out in the open, I felt both elation and fear. What had I done?

Permissions

GRATEFUL ACKNOWLEDGEMENT IS MADE TO the following sources for permission to reprint from previously published material.

Quotation from the song "Falling in Love with Love" by Richard Rodgers and Lorez Hart, © 1938, Williamson Music, A Division of Rodger & Hammerstein: An Imagem Company; co-publisher: WB Music Corp and Alfred Music Publishing Co., Inc. Reprinted by permission.

The quotations from poems by Patrick Kavanagh are reprinted from *Collected Poems* edited by Antoinette Quinn (Allen Lane, 2004) by kind permission of the Trustees of the Estate of the late Katherine B. Kavanagh, through the Jonathan Williams Literary Agency.

Excerpt from Murphy, © 1938 by the Estate of Samuel Beckett. Used by permission of Grove/Atlantic, Inc.

Quotations from the poems "Ash Wednesday" and "The Love-song of J. Alfred Prufrock" by T.S. Eliot are from *Collected Poems 1909–1962* by T.S. Eliot. Reprinted by kind permission of Faber & Faber Ltd.

"The First Elegy" translated by Stephen Mitchell, © 1982 by Stephen Mitchell, "The Second Elegy", translated by Stephen Mitchell, © 1982 by Stephen Mitchell, "The Third Elegy", translated by Stephen Mitchell, "The Fourth Elegy", translated by Stephen Mitchell, from *The Selected Poetry of Rainer*